Would Mao
Hold Bitcoin?

Would Mao Hold Bitcoin?

The Past, Present, and Future of
Bitcoin in Techo-Nationalist China

Roger Huang

Foreword by Alex Gladstein

BITCOIN MAGAZINE
≡III BOOKS™
Bitcoin Magazine Books
Nashville, TN

ISBN 979-8-9891326-5-2 (Paperback)
ISBN 979-8-9891326-6-9 (eBook)

BITCOIN MAGAZINE
≋Ⅲ BOOKS™

Published by Bitcoin Magazine Books
An imprint of BTC Media, LLC
300 10th Avenue South, Nashville, TN 37203

Address all queries to contact@btcmedia.org

Interior design by MediaNeighbours.com

To my parents

To my community—the friends and supporters who made this possible

Contents

Foreword

Roger Huang has written a uniquely insightful book about money, control, China's role in the history of currency and—surprisingly enough—in Bitcoin.

Today, the Chinese Communist Party are known as "currency manipulators," famous for keeping the RMB weak over the past few decades to boost exports in order to become the world's manufacturing factory for everything.

But hundreds of years ago, as Huang explains, Chinese emperors made even bigger changes to the medium of money. First, by minting coins backed by precious metals, and then, later, in the time of the Mongols, removing that backing, leading to printing massive sums of paper notes. The ensuing hyperinflation would end one empire and start another.

In more recent history, in the early 20th century, inflation would lead to the end of the Nationalist project in China, with frustration over carrying clumps of useless notes in wheelbarrows leading in part to the rise of Mao Zedong and the Communist project. Mao's inner circle called inflation the "scourge of capitalism" and turned to organized force to tame the rising cost of living.

The Chairman tried to keep inflation down through violence by imposing consumption limits, price controls, and strict social norms around spending. When these controls were eventually lifted, inflation spiked again, and this led in part to the social frustrations that boiled over into Tiananmen Square. One can argue that the struggle over inflation has defined the last millennia of Chinese politics.

Over the past thirty years, the most recent Chinese leaders, including "emperor" Xi Jinping, have pursued what Huang calls a "techno-nationalist" policy, seeking to use cutting-edge technology to cement control and surveillance over the world's largest population. The idea is essentially that it's ok for citizens to take advantage of the capitalist system, to live long and prosper, as long as they don't criticize the government. As soon as they do, it's all over.

The CCP uses new tools like AI surveillance, social credit, and Central Bank Digital Currencies to try and keep itself afloat in an increasingly electronic age. In a way, Xi Jinping is trying to do what Mao did, except by replacing some of the violence with technology, replacing police with self-police and thought-police.

If techno-nationalism is Xi Jinping's thesis, then Huang shows that Bitcoin is the antithesis. He paints a vivid story of China's paradoxical role in the rise of Bitcoin, as the birthplace of mining, with the two largest miners and mining pools originating in China, and the largest early exchanges originating in China. Fast forward to 2024 and the largest cryptocurrency exchange in the world, Binance, was founded in China, by a person whose father had fled the cultural revolution for being too much of an intellectual.

In the same way, Huang tells us, Bitcoin has for the most part been chased out of China. Binance has since been banned, while F2Pool and AntPool now operate outside the country. Intense controls have been placed on the ability of citizens to exchange RMB for BTC, and mining has formally been banned. Bitcoin still survives, but in an underground network of P2P markets and minimalist message boards. The largest Mandarin-language Bitcoin podcast operates outside of the country. Abroad, Tiananmen Square survivors have raised money for projects in Bitcoin, while their names and presence are forbidden on the mainland.

In the following pages, Huang will take you on a fascinating ride through the centuries and decades, showing how Chinese history teaches us much about the choice now in front of world leaders today.

Do they try and emulate Xi Jinping, and create an economy of control? Huang says that "Bitcoin offers a backdoor for individuals within a country, and ultimately, countries themselves, to break" from this framework. But will they follow that?

What is certain is that the Chinese Communist Party, in its current form, would be against a Bitcoin standard. The CCP needs censorship, control, and closed capital markets to survive. Bitcoin is the complete opposite: free speech, private property, and open capital markets.

So will the CCP succeed in squashing Bitcoin, cutting itself off from the outside world? Or will Bitcoin survive, growing slowly but inevitably as a resistance economy inside China?

The first step to knowing is reading this book.

—Alex Gladstein, April 2024

Introduction

I wrote *Would Mao Hold Bitcoin?* because I thought the intersection between Bitcoin and China contained one of the most meaningful paradoxes of the 21st century—one that had a major impact on people's wallets and freedoms while being largely underreported. I'd been writing about the topic for many years, and being part of many discussions about both Bitcoin and China, I saw a unique opportunity to combine areas of research that had been a passion and a large part of my life. I'd written about Bitcoin as early as 2014 with TechCrunch and VentureBeat, and my bylines on China spanned the *Toronto Star* to the *Los Angeles Review of Books*.

Would Mao Hold Bitcoin? covers why the Chinese people are so interested in Bitcoin while the Chinese government is so adamant about trying to ban it. The book does this by breaking down China's recent history, the ideology and practical effects of the bans China has tried to implement, as well as the central bank digital currency it has tried to champion with the Digital yuan as a response to Bitcoin. It contains character stories and anecdotes about the Chinese Bitcoin scene, where the world's largest mining companies and exchanges initially grew. It also profiles people trying to circumvent the techno-nationalist surveillance and control apparatus the Chinese party-state has built, and what that means as China is looking to spread its model throughout the world.

Bitcoin has been shaped by its interaction with the Chinese state and the Chinese people. Many prominent Bitcoin businesses were built by Chinese nationals, and Bitcoin really grew up from a small child that helped people exchange pizza for Internet money to a mature monetary network within a Chinese context. China's attempts to ban Bitcoin and replace it with central bank digital currency have spurred a movement of awareness for decentralized freedom-tech as well as several other unforeseen consequences.

I've lived through some of that disconnect myself and found hope in the areas where freedom-tech has helped bridge the gap. While the Chinese Internet was banning apps as innocuous as LinkedIn for being American, and had long banned Clubhouse from its app store, people from Mainland China were communicating quite freely on Nostr. And for different transfers of value, Bitcoin and Lightning Network have helped make payments possible where no other tool could.

The book isn't just my personal journey however. *Would Mao Hold Bitcoin?* is also a philosophical exploration about a coming conflict—namely, as humanity progresses and expands our technological capability to do more, are we ok with permitting states, restrained more by capability than law, to follow and enforce new boundaries on individual freedoms? China and its series of bans on Bitcoin and adjacent technologies, as well as the fostering of technologies that increase "social trust" like blockchain and central bank digital currencies, offers a space that not only defines this conflict but a prime opportunity for reflection: unfamiliar enough to foster learning, but familiar enough to be able to grasp the thread of where it'll all go.

I hope that readers like you will leave this book more aware of the historical, technical, and social factors shaping the strange union between Bitcoin and China—and why that debate matters to your wallets and your freedoms. Mostly though, I hope that you are empowered to be an active participant in the discussion between the technologies used to empower you and the technologies your government will use to try to control you.

—Roger Huang

Chapter One

The Black and White Cat

Although Bitcoin first appeared in 2009, the history of China is essential for truly understanding it. The sweeping history of the Chinese people's relationships with emperors, warlords, and the Communist ruling class has shaped a long and nuanced relationship between state power and the people's trust in its money. As a result, in China inflation is more than just a point in a Bitcoin post or a narrow reference to Venezuela or Weimar Germany. It is a potent force that is alive and has deposed some of the largest and most powerful empires known to humanity.

China's history contains essential patterns that help explain the unique rise of Bitcoin within the emergence of China's techno-nationalism. Inflation and the wheelbarrows of Nationalist Party money helped turn the tide toward Communist one-party rule under Mao. Inflation also helped spur the Tiananmen protests that almost ended the Chinese Communist Party's rule and colored the fight for the Chinese Communist Party's soul after the Cultural Revolution killed millions. And fear of inflation led the party to encourage Chinese entrepreneurs and investors to shift from espousing socialist principles to embrace a "socialism with Chinese characteristics"—an economic policy that would both help Bitcoin grow from a gangly teenager to a mature financial product while also leading to bans that would change both Bitcoin and China.

China's History and Inflation

Bitcoin is known by many for its association with inflation and decentralization. One of the first things that resonates with people is the 21 million Bitcoin cap. Next is the idea of money without the state. In China, both resonate because of its particular history.

Inflation played a crucial role in the downfall of Nationalist-ruled China and the ascent of the Chinese Communist Party. Propagandists for the Chinese Communist Party portrayed inflation as a "scourge of capitalism."[1] For twenty years during Mao's rule, prices for everyday goods and commodities remained constant, though access to those goods was hard to maintain through the Great Chinese Famine and the Cultural Revolution. But in fact as far back as the Mongol-ruled yuan Dynasty, hyperinflating paper money caused the fall of regimes in China.

China's financial system initially began with tangible-backed goods as the basis of currency. Over time, the nature of the backing evolved, from cowrie shells being shipped from the Maldives[2] around 1000 BC to gold being issued as the "upper currency" by Qin Shi Huang, China's "first emperor."[3] By the Tang Dynasty (which emerged around the same time as the decline of the Western Roman Empire in the West), credit systems were well-established, with *feiqian* or "money on the fly"[4] and shops dedicated to safeguarding money. Fast forward several centuries to when the heirs of Genghis Khan founded the yuan Dynasty. While rulers like Kublai Khan initially issued coins with backing from precious metals, government spending eventually grew to the degree where non-backed paper money was needed to keep up with the expenses, leading to the collapse of the regime. The damage assigned to this fiat money failure was part of the reason the rulers of the Ming Dynasty were able to ascend and replace the yuan.

While Nationalist leader Chiang Kai-Shek insisted that it was the Soviet Union's backing of the Chinese Communist Party that ensured its victory, it was also the mismanagement of the country under the Nationalist Party that made it ripe for revolution—"most evident in the runaway inflation of such staggering proportions that city dwellers sometimes needed wheelbarrows full of nearly worthless currency to buy rice."[5] After periods where the Chinese currency was pegged to either gold, silver, or foreign currencies such as the Pound or the US Dollar, Mao started his reign in 1948 with the new yuan, "the standard of currency for a New China."[6] China's central bank, The People's Bank of China, was founded on December 1st, 1948, after Mao consolidated several regional monetary authorities. The new yuan would be paper money backed by cotton instead of hard commodities.

For Mao, who always considered his winning of China from Chiang Kai-Shek a cornerstone achievement, avoiding inflation was an important mission—even if it meant banning most, if not all, of private enterprise in pursuit of a "utopian" socialist state. For the better part of three decades, the Chinese Communist Party kept inflation down not by pegging its new paper currency to another standard, but rather by imposing brute force on the Chinese people and creating a system where fidelity to the state, price quotas, and strict consumption were enforced with differing degrees of re-education, political violence, and leadership-as-cult. Paper money enabled the Communist Party to take over and remold the Chinese state to its liking—a coupling so long entwined that most academics now describe China's governance as being the Chinese party-state.

Deng and the Era of Reform

The Cultural Revolution was Mao's last-ditch attempt to shape his succession. He rallied young radicals in his cult of personality to "bombard the center" and attack "capitalist-roaders" while destroying the "Four Olds." University-age youths were sent down to the countryside to work and toil on the farms. The Red Guards proceeded to condemn class enemies, often killing them, and even desecrated the tomb of Confucius. Millions died during the decade the Cultural Revolution lasted. During this time, his heir apparent, Liu Shaoqi, fell out of favor and was tortured to death in a secret prison. Nuclear engineers, writers, and many of China's leading cultural lights were killed or committed suicide. By the end of the Cultural Revolution, Shanghai's Conservatory of Music, once one of Asia's first orchestras, had no playable pianos. Its halls would gradually fill with memorials to the twenty professors, spouses, and students who lost their lives during the Cultural Revolution.[7]

When Mao Zedong died in 1978, his legacy was at stake, as his death opened up the avenue for a new generation of leadership to rise. But his heirs would not be the ones he chose. The comrades that emerged were drawn from the ranks of the purged. One of those leaders was Deng Xiaoping, who survived the deep scars of the Cultural Revolution. Another was Zhao Ziyang, who was to become his premier.

As one of his first acts as *de facto* paramount leader after Mao's death, Deng declared an age of opening and reform. The trauma and destruction of the Cultural Revolution had just begun to scar, but China had yet to emerge from its economic slumber. GDP per capita was about $175 (denominated in 2010 dollars), while in the US it was more than $10,000—50 times higher. China was just a generation away from acute poverty and famine, but even now, endemic deprivation reigned. However, Deng had a plan—and a metaphor in mind. He boldly declared that it "doesn't matter whether it's a black cat or a white cat. So long as it catches mice, it's a good cat." This signaled a total change in mentality for the Chinese ruling party, which under Mao had created a system where you could be imprisoned or worse for holding "capitalist beliefs." Under Deng to be rich was "glorious." China no longer imprisoned capitalists and landlords, but rather pursued "socialism with Chinese characteristics"—a form of state-managed capitalism that permitted private wealth so long as it built toward the Communist Party's absolute political control.

Deng put his faith in the Special Economic Zones and encouraged new goods and capital inflow from abroad. In the 1980s, most people knew Shenzhen as a sleepy fishing village, but a decade later became one of the first cities to define China's growth and its greater integration into the world economy. While Shenzhen was the first

Special Economic Zone, others soon followed in coastal cities across the mainland. These Special Economic Zones became a model for economic growth and liberalization. Today, Shenzhen is a metonym for the Chinese technology industry, championed as the center of technological innovation and is one of the highest GDP per capita areas in the People's Republic of China. It is both a metaphor and an emblem of China's economic rise and China's aspiration for its economic model.

Shenzhen's residents see the US-China tech war and the proxy conflicts between those two powers as boiling down to a fight between the vibrant urban villages of Shenzhen's tech sector and the San Francisco Bay Area.[8] With the Greater Pearl Bay Area, an effort to unite Macau, Hong Kong, Guangzhou, and Shenzhen, the Chinese party-state wants to surpass the American megapolis surrounding the San Francisco to San Jose corridor that became the world's preeminent tech hub. However, the economic reforms and the beginnings of China's techno-nationalist rise that created the foundations for China to become the world's largest Bitcoin mining hub did not come without costs: the Chinese people bore the brunt of increasing prices beyond their control, which caused a backlash against political reform.

After Mao Zedong died, Chinese politics split into two broad factions. One faction believed in some combination of political and economic reform. Headlining this faction were Zhao Ziyang and Hu Yaobang. These reformists wanted to move as quickly as possible away from Maoist-era economic controls and even flirted with the possibility of ending one-party rule. In the aftermath of the Cultural

Revolution, Zhao Ziyang enjoyed remarkable success as governor of Sichuan province, removing restrictions on private enterprises and seeing wealth grow. He was known as someone to look for if you wanted to find food—perhaps the highest compliment you could pay someone in a country that had gone through several rounds of famine.

Opposed to the reformists were the conservatives, headed by the Eight Elders, who were also determined to move the system forward from Mao but not from the socialism he championed. The Eight Elders were named after the Eight Immortals, Taoist deities. One of the Eight Elders, Chen Yun, claimed he would have "defected" to the Nationalists long ago if he had known how Mao's rule would turn out. However, his instincts told him not to move far from Mao's socialist state. He decried the inflation that came with economic reform and thought it was a non-starter to shift from one-party rule.

Deng Xiaoping was in the middle. The "paramount leader" notably refused to call himself that due to fears of returning the country to Mao-era cultism. Instead, he worked behind the scenes, assuaging the tensions in both factions, and at times helping one side or another as China became enmeshed in a fundamental conflict: how to move on from Maoism while inheriting Mao's legacy to continue the nation-state.

While this new generation of Chinese leadership was finding its bearings after one-man rule, a spike in inflation after economic reforms led to political momentum against the party. By 1984 Deng had grown impatient with China being in the middle when it came to price reform and elevated it to the top of the political agenda. However, it wasn't until 1988 that the full effect of this directive would come into view. That year the Chinese government announced the lifting of price controls, some effectively overnight, which led to a spate of panic buying. Goods flew off the shelf. In Harbin, the northern city of China known for being a gateway for Soviet-Chinese cooperation, there was a bank run followed by a massive spending spree. In the span of just one month, the largest department store in the city sold about $300,000 USD worth of electrical appliances—a fortune at the time and almost 200 times the monthly average spent.

The actions of Harbin's residents foreshadowed what would happen across the country. During this time, the largest bank run in Communist Party history occurred.[9] The Chinese people feared that their meager savings would quickly get eroded by inflation and tried to withdraw their paper money to spend it as quickly as possible before it was worth less. They weren't wrong: prior to 1988, inflation in China had grown about 7.5% every year, but in 1988, there was suddenly an 18.5% increase.[10] What happened in China in 1988 echoes what happens to weak currencies around the world—from Lebanon to Argentina—that are at the periphery of the US dollar-ordered financial system.[11] The bank run not only threatened to undo the price reforms and private banking system that were supposed to be the foundation of the Chinese Communist Party's new stance toward private wealth, they also threatened the Chinese party-state's very mandate to rule.

Tiananmen Square and the End of Political Reform

The overheated inflation in the summer of 1988 also had long-standing consequences for the fight between economic reformers like Zhao Ziyang and the conservatives he faced. The inflationary consequences of price reform led to Zhao Ziyang's retreat from economic policymaking and his ultimate undoing,[12] leading to the transfer of political legitimacy from the reformers to a faction headed by Premier Li Peng, who tended to be more conservative and was aligned with the Eight Elders. It marked the end of the hope of political reform with economic reform. It also marked the beginning of a Chinese tragedy: the crackdown on the Tiananmen Square protests and the ensuing massacre, which would ultimately be authorized by Premier Peng.

The protests in Tiananmen Square were the flashpoint between these two factions. It drove a wedge inside the Communist Party between the reformers who wanted economic and political liberalization and the conservatives who wanted a more robust economy for China without any of the attendant democratization that might happen. The protests marked an existential fight for the soul of the party: whether political development could co-exist with financial development or be divorced, and whether the party could embrace capitalistic practices or be destroyed by them. The threat that grew from the Tiananmen movement particularly resonated within the Communist Party, which had always prided itself on its ability to join and mobilize the working class with intellectual elites. Tiananmen Square grew out of the nexus of students protesting after the death of the reformer Hu Yaobang, Zhao Ziyang's mentor, but it soon encompassed working class solidarity, bloodshed, and enforced amnesia. It was accelerated by the unease the working class felt about their new circumstances: seeing the paper cotton yuan that Mao had enforced with blood become tattered with new price reforms.

The party's response to what it felt like was another Cultural Revolution in the making was utter horror. An editorial from the China Communist Youth League advocated a stark response, ushering in a transition from the party's time as a revolutionary party to one where it would control economic assets and large parts of the Chinese economy it was developing.[13] The rhetoric between students and party members sharpened until Zhao Ziyang came to Tiananmen Square to tell the students that it was too late. The central leadership, scarred by their experience with the Cultural Revolution, had decided to use the military to quash the Tiananmen protests.

Years later, Lu Xun's words about the political massacre in the halls of Chinese power still resonate: "Lies written in ink cannot disguise facts written in blood." Though the Chinese party-state has tried its best to repress this version of history, Tiananmen Square and its discussion is now a stark battlefront in the controlled Internet that the Chinese party-state curates and the sharing of information on "freedom-tech" adjacent tools, like Nostr and Bitcoin-based communities.

After Tiananmen Square, the powers-that-be confined Zhao Ziyang to house arrest for the rest of his days. The factions that endured still contested the need for political and economic reform, but the space accorded to the debate narrowed. Political reform and a shift away from one-party rule were seen as dead on arrival, while economic reform would proceed more slowly than before. This is a spiritual and ideological contest that plays out every day in a party stuck between serving markets in a socialist manner and in the extension of the "One Country, Two Systems" model the Chinese party-state champions to absorb nearby regions such as Hong Kong. Many of the children of the party elite that ordered the massacre around Tiananmen Square rule today and have an essential part in the economic and political fabric of China.

One of the sons of Chen Yun, who ardently opposed political reforms and the Tiananmen Square protests—and who helped author a part of the anti-democratic Chinese Communist Youth League editorial—was Chen yuan. He became the vice governor of the People's Bank of China in 1988, right at the time it became a modern central bank and took on foreign reserves. He was one of the first officials in the People's Bank of China who could speak English in the 1990s,[14] part of a new generation of Chinese leadership that looked to embrace the West despite conservative and ideological roots that feared it. He would later become chairman of the China Development Bank, which helped create the local financing required to power China's economy through investment, with marquee projects such as the Three Gorges Dam and Shanghai's Pudong International Airport in its portfolio. Current Chinese General Secretary and paramount leader Xi Jinping is a product of this intergenerational power transfer as well.

The earlier generation of Chinese leadership—the first to embrace Communist rule without Mao—had been stuck with a terrible paradox. Many of them had suffered immensely under Mao, forced into prison or exile, and birthed children with those lessons in mind. They recognized that the Cultural Revolution he had unleashed had caused terrible damage to the People's Republic of China. However, they had also inherited a barely surviving yet coherent nation-state upon which they could put their dreams. So they decided to repudiate Mao's legacy privately, especially in matters of economic policy, while publicly upholding the man who had built the nation they hoped to inherit.

The next generation of leaders did the same as Deng—erasing the legacy of blood that flowed at Tiananmen Square in order to ensure the survival of the Chinese Communist Party and continue the one-party project. The revolutionary party Mao had created would now be the party of stability and harmony: the revolution had been won. There would be no need for Mao to hold Bitcoin if he were still at the helm of one-party rule.

Economic Revival in Post-Deng China

Inflation matters to the Chinese Communist Party as much as it matters to Bitcoiners because of this history. China's party-state elite have tried to show that they are the best governing force to rein in this economic sin while permitting wealth to grow for Chinese families, ridiculing the West at times for its liberal monetary policies. During this post-Deng period, speculation by the Chinese retail investor class began in earnest, and the chase for private wealth was kickstarted under the watch of the party. Real estate purchases were allowed, and the Chinese banking sector allowed foreign banks to conduct RMB business. Though this journey was beset with problems as it was in the 1980s (for example, the 1997 Asian Financial Crisis), it marked a change in China's economic direction.

In 2001, the People's Republic of China joined the World Trade Organization and officially broke bread with the

American-led international trade order—a change that corresponded with the handover of power between Li Peng, the hardline premier who was the most visible figure in encouraging state violence and the violent crackdown on the Tiananmen Square protests, and Zhu Rongji, an economic pragmatist and more aligned with reform.

Under Zhu Rongji's watch, the party liberalized certain parts of the Chinese economy and sold off certain state-owned firms to fit the new direction the Chinese party-state wanted. It also created the patronage and income system that has led to China's high-income inequality, as rural residents are priced out in order to make way for flashy property developments. The United States put sanctions on China during this period—many of them based on an executive order signed by Bill Clinton in the aftermath of the Tiananmen Square Massacre, where trade with China had to be subject to China meeting specific human rights metrics and benchmarks. Even though its WTO's ascension required China to liberalize its economy, it was a needed step for the Chinese party-state to be able to export products to the United States. This helped China become the manufacturing engine that powered American consumption and started it down its own development path—a "quiet" path that Hu Jintao and Wen Jiabao's leadership generation would follow.

The Chinese Communist Party worked diligently at this time to bide its strength and integrate with the global trade system captained by the United States. The story they sold was quite simple: China could peacefully rise within the established world order. It would export cheaply manufactured goods to the United States, allowing the American consumer engine that powered the world to enjoy the benefits of reduced wages in another country. Then, it would invest the dollars received from Chinese exports back into the American financial system, whether through treasuries or other ventures.

China initially aimed to replicate the Asian Tigers—manufacturing-led, export-oriented growth coupled with economic and political controls. The Chinese party-state found inspiration in Singapore, where heavy-handed government action on protests and union strikes combined with free-market adventurism. Deng's relationship with Singapore's founder and leader, Lee Kuan Yew, was solid, and Singapore's development model directly inspired the Chinese party-state as it grew.[15] China's techno-nationalist project could also take some inspiration from South Korea's path from military dictatorship and cloistered corporate elites to a modern economic power.

However, China's development model still begs the ultimate question: could lasting economic benefit come without political reform? Could the Chinese people be satisfied with stable economic gains even if they did not have political rights? South Korea had to democratize to persist in its economic gains. Taiwan was once ruled under martial law by the Nationalist government that was exiled by Mao, but in 1994, following student protests, Taiwanese elections became open and contested, and soon the opposition Democratic Progressive Party started winning elections.

Conclusion: Bitcoin Through the Lens of China's Past

In sum, China's long history with paper money—the longest among all states—doesn't just offer an informative history lesson. It gives China a fascinating role in the fight for the future as it seeks to extend this legacy to electronic money and define state standards for the money of the future. It explains why Chinese people were uniquely fascinated by Bitcoin and became some of Bitcoin's biggest investors and entrepreneurs.

In his novel *1984,* Orwell wrote, "To understand the past is to control the future." The story of how China met Bitcoin did not begin in 2009, after the Great Financial Recession that struck the West and when Satoshi created Bitcoin. It began much earlier with a clash of ideas, one born after the Great Recession and the other out of the ashes of the Cultural Revolution. After Maoism faltered, Deng's state capitalist model, "socialism with Chinese characteristics," became the new norm. Inflation split the party into two: reformers who wanted political and economic change, and conservatives who wanted state capitalism and absolute political control. Tiananmen ensured that the conservatives would win and that their faction would lead China's techno-nationalist rise to become the second-largest economy in the world.

But if China's techno-nationalist rise is the thesis, then Bitcoin is its antithesis. It is no coincidence that a techno-nationalist state whose rise is based on leapfrog technologies is so advanced in setting standards for central bank electronic cash—a future Bitcoiners wanted to avoid. Indeed, from inflation to political repression, the very nature of the Chinese party-state has created the conditions for its oppositional force—Bitcoin.

While Satoshi's reference point was the Great Financial Recession that was striking the West, his creation would graph itself upon an ascendant techno-nationalist power, insecure about a past marked by forced amnesia, bloodshed, revolution, doubting both truth and foreign influences, and fearing most of all the hidden factor behind much of it: inflation and trust in the state itself. China's unique history in the 20th century has shaped China's relationship with Bitcoin—and forged the mixed lines between individuals and the collective that explain why some of the most active builders in Bitcoin have come from a country that would eventually ban it.

Chapter Two

Bitcoin Through Chinese Eyes

Bitcoin is a character in one of the most fascinating contrasts of the 21st century, and to understand its role requires a deeper understanding of its culture, history, and mechanics before we can understand why it was so attractive to Chinese entrepreneurs and investors while being derided by the Chinese state. What the Chinese people think about Bitcoin, the interplay between Bitcoin culture and China, as well as how Chinese people buy Bitcoin all play a critical role in understanding the future of Bitcoin and China.

The Chinese people have had a nuanced relationship with Bitcoin. Bitcoin is "magic Internet money." Bitcoin is a million people with red-eye avatars on Twitter. Above all, Bitcoin, especially when combined with China, is a confusing topic. After all, isn't China creating a "cryptocurrency" of sorts in some variant of the digital yuan? And what really is a blockchain or cryptocurrency? Is China or other nefarious state-actors using Bitcoin in order to undermine the United States? Getting to the bottom of these questions will take time and requires starting with a fundamental understanding of the technology.

Bitcoin as Technology in China

States create and maintain financial value: the bills that you hold come with the fiat conviction that a state with enough force to drive taxation backs it. This is a key distinction because Bitcoin is often described as being "backed by nothing." Yet that's not entirely true: what Bitcoin does and how it functions allows for the expression of cross-border value while going outside the traditional central banking and retail banking system that usually distributes money supply within each country.

Decentralization is having a transparent and public ledger for financial value that doesn't rely on the interaction of private, trust-based ledgers that represent deposits at a bank—a system that ultimately ladders up to a governance model where a central bank controls currency, and savings are placed in virtual accounts that are outside of an individual's direct control and can be censored as needed. Without that need for differentiated governance (i.e., who really runs the chain?), blockchains are just extravagant data structures that cost extra energy and time. At its core, Bitcoin is a public ledger that uses private and public keys to transmit something of value between different addresses without anybody being able to stop that transaction from happening. Every transaction is transparent and validated by many nodes that broadcast the valid state of the system to each other. That's the technology: however, the effect is to create a system that goes outside nation-state frameworks of violence, taxation, and bank corporations to allow people to trade value with each other. The effect is currency without the state.

Bitcoin's mining algorithm scales in difficulty and responds to the amount of computing power devoted to the system. The system was designed for laptops to be able to mine, but in practice, large-scale public corporations and even governments are the ones that do most of the mining. Often Bitcoin mining converges in places with cheap power and (some) regulatory certainty. It uses specialized computing chips called ASICs (application-specific integrated circuits). ASICs are built for specific and intensive applications—and for Bitcoin mining, there are two companies that have a duopoly: BitMain and MicroBTC. Both were founded by Chinese citizens and started off as Chinese companies. Their hardware now controls a large portion of the Bitcoin mining market.

Some people think China is behind Bitcoin, notably Palantir co-founder Peter Thiel.[16] The fact that Chinese companies make Bitcoin mining equipment is a factor in how Bitcoin runs. Trump-level taxes on Chinese technology imports hurt American Bitcoin mining companies trying to import either BitMain or MicroBTC equipment— any future tariffs are likely to have the same effect.[17] And because China and Taiwan dominate semiconductor manufacturing, Bitcoin and other networks reliant on computing equipment have an analog bottleneck: the factories and foundries in East Asia that produce the computing power needed to protect Bitcoin through mining. Decentralization is an ideal, and Bitcoin is tending toward it. But mining hardware concentration is one slight barrier and a source of concentration and centralization. After China's Bitcoin mining ban, the amount of computing power dedicated to protecting Bitcoin increased but was more geographically spread, with the largest Bitcoin mining pool now head-quartered in the United States.

Bitcoin as a Topic in China

But Bitcoin isn't just a financial and mining technology. It also aggregates a network of contributors and believers. This is perhaps one of its most interesting elements: com-munities and independent media sources tend to pop up. There is *Bitcoin Magazine*, where Vitalik Buterin first formed his thoughts on Ethereum. There are Bitcoin-related and Bitcoin-only events. Indeed, Bitcoin was founded on a cryp-tography mailing list—a remnant of an era where open-source coders were considering what to do in the face of export bans on cryptography technology. The grassroots of Bitcoin matters for the movement as much as the price.

Within the People's Republic of China, Hong Kong, and Macau, many groups and associations have been dedi-cated to studying Bitcoin and its potential effects on the Chinese economy and the rest of the world. One example is the Bitcoin Association of Hong Kong, which helped cre-ate event spaces and created policy papers on emerging issues for Bitcoin. The movement of these groups has also reflected broader trends in Bitcoin's relationship with the People's Republic of China. Certain Bitcoin conferences had to flee the mainland in order to host events, sometimes under short notice due to sudden shifts in central bank or party-state policies and positions toward Bitcoin. This mirrors what happened to exchanges that had to migrate due to the crackdowns on the mainland.[18]

There were previously Meetup groups dedicated to Bitcoin from Beijing to Shenzhen, but lately there hasn't been as much activity in these groups: for example, the Beijing Meetup last had a public event in 2019.[19] Whether that's because of darkening sentiment against Bitcoin or COVID-19 restrictions, it shows that there used to be more community events and a more active Bitcoin community—even if that activity seems to have paused now.

On Meetup.com (which would skew more toward English-speaking expats), there are 25 cryptocurrency groups in China with 6,500 members –a drop in the ocean when you think about the number of people in the People's Republic of China, but an impressive showing nevertheless for a technology that is so oft-frowned upon by the authorities. A diversity of cryptocurrencies exist among the Meetup groups, with a division often noted between Bitcoin meetups and more Ethereum-focused meetups. Pockets of the Chinese Internet have debated back and forth on the merits of both, and the "maxi" conversation—the idea that some people who support Bitcoin are "Bitcoin maximalist" extremists who do not see value in other cryptocurrencies—exists in China just as it does elsewhere.

One thing to notice is regional trends: the largest Bitcoin Meetup is in Beijing, while the largest Ethereum Meetup is in Shanghai. This isn't a coincidence: NFTs and Ethereum have gotten more traction in Shanghai, where the tech sector is more focused on e-commerce and products, while Beijing hosts a vast amount of state investment in hard tech, creating the conditions for a technology sector with holistic interests despite its proximity to the seat of power in China. China's current events and conferences are now much more focused on blockchain per the state's primal focus on implementing "blockchain" rather than cryptocurrencies or Bitcoin.[20] This is a result of marketing hype and the Chinese party-state's support behind developing "blockchain" patents, which feeds into the official environment of support for "blockchain" events while simultaneously discouraging events related to "speculative" technologies such as Bitcoin. While there used to be Bitcoin conferences in mainland China, different sources conceded they hadn't heard of anything or been to one from 2021 onwards.

Bitcoin mining conferences used to take place actively in mainland China. This was until the central Chinese authorities decided to impose guidance asking for provinces to ban Bitcoin mining. Miners then packed up their equipment and headed to other destinations (from Texas to neighboring Kazakhstan) or went into hiding. Bitmain and MicroBT, the world's two largest Bitcoin mining chip producers, have moved their events elsewhere since at least 2020. Bitmain held its 2023 gathering in Hong Kong.[21]

One marker of the grassroots movement is the number of people who run Bitcoin and Lightning nodes. As of October 2023, there were 49 people running Bitcoin full nodes with Chinese IP addresses recorded. Bitcoin full nodes can be run on any computing device that has an Internet connection. One popular "off-the-shelf" implementation is based off the Raspberry PI (Umbrel), but there are plenty of ways to run a node on any plain desktop or laptop lying around— so long as it's expected to be powered on 24/7.

Bitcoin full nodes validate and transmit information on all of the blocks and transactions that are passing through the Bitcoin network. They are truly a marker for Bitcoin's "you contribute, you belong" culture. While some confer privacy benefits and miners use some to track Bitcoin and the blocks they mine extra carefully, there are also people running Bitcoin as just a way to contribute to its open-source development around the world—similar but even more expanded than people who run Tor networks that allow others to browse the web privately if they so wish. That there are still people willing to run Bitcoin full nodes with Chinese IP addresses and networks shows that Bitcoin can still persist in countries where there are multiple censorship attempts.

Some coders contribute code to Bitcoin Core and adjacent products and layers such as Lightning Network and Nostr. There are technical members of the community who translate Bitcoin documents into Mandarin. Most of the Bitcoin Core team and its key members are in the United States, yet grants have been provided in the past by Chinese-based organizations like OKCoin, showing the global nature of Bitcoin.[22]

What Do the Chinese People Say About Bitcoin?

Chinese people in tech havens and those overseas express their opinions openly. Information spread about Bitcoin early, helping to spur the initial entrepreneurs who helped consolidate Bitcoin mining in the People's Republic of China when it was nascent. The Internet cafes that powered gaming across major urban centers were stocked well with GPUs that could be used to mine Bitcoin.[23] Resources in Mandarin began to pop up early, focused on how to mine for this new idea. For some, the appeal was the money. For others, the appeal was the idea of government-less money—and a path to freedom.

The Mandarin-language version of Bitcoin's description for Wikipedia is quite robust, though Wikipedia is censored in the People's Republic of China, meaning most Mandarin readers in the mainland will be unlikely to have access to this information. There is a Bitcoin entry in Baike, which is Baidu's version of Wikipedia, one of the largest Mandarin-language encyclopedias—so it isn't as if the whole concept itself is being completely wiped from memory.[24] Most searches for Bitcoin in Mandarin on Google's services return overseas websites with English translations instead of anything that is written within domestic Chinese borders.

The Baike entry is quite robust. It links to related articles that are mostly exchange-related. Unlike others set through fiat standards, Bitcoin is described as a currency that uses algorithmic means to determine its distribution. The Satoshi origin story starts the entry and both the peer-to-peer and decentralized nature of Bitcoin come to the fore. Under the Baike entry there is a "TaShuo" section, meaning "They Say," a place where contributors from across the Chinese Internet can create articles and content on the topic. Most of these discussions are about technical analysis of the price level of Bitcoin. There is for example an article from CryptoXiaoYa (Crypto "small elegant"—a Mandarin way to describe, since dynastic times, a young, beautiful female) about the price level of Bitcoin and where it might go given network activity. This isn't so dissimilar from the "West," where endless content is made about the current price level of 24/7 updated Bitcoin markets and where opinions are voiced from everywhere on whether Bitcoin might go up or down.

The social networks within the Chinese Internet are vast. Those bridging between the diaspora and the Chinese Internet might use Discord and Facebook. WeChat might seem like an "everything app" to some, but the reality is that there are many different social communities. Xiaohongshu (小红书) is a cross between Instagram and Pinterest. While appealing mostly to young professionals, it hosts content that connects aspiring Chinese students and Western jobs as well as various Internet memes. There is a considerable amount of financial advice and analysis, and while still subject to the same regulations and rules as any Chinese Internet app (for example, as of 2022, it's impossible to access it with a VPN on). Bitcoin is discussed more openly here than you might expect, although Xiaohongshu is probably the most "Western-friendly" of all of the Chinese Internet's platforms. There's technical analysis and talk about the price action of Bitcoin. As a financial asset, Bitcoin news tends to move the same way in both the Chinese Internet and the "Western" Internet. The price level and action are what drive quick-hit news, especially on platforms that aim for quick engagement and clicks. A large portion of Mandarin-language material on Bitcoin in these forums is based on technical analysis of Bitcoin and altcoins like it. Some of the basics of this can be explained in a quick summary: technical analysis involves a deep reading of charts and daily trading patterns. Somebody can glance at how a chart is moving and supply/demand levels without integrating macroeconomic knowledge or deducing what is happening outside of the chart. This is the majority of the chatter on Bitcoin and shows how important in China price is to Bitcoin.

Clubhouse conversations have in the past featured Chinese Ethereum users showing up with their Bored Ape profile pictures, bemoaning the "toxic" nature of Bitcoin maximalism. Public Telegram groups that claim to represent Bitcoin in China have in practice become a series of pinned articles and promotions of altcoins—and perhaps a way for the group admin to make a quick buck. Overall, the "cryptocurrency" conversations in the People's Republic of China seem more geared toward the speculative side of Bitcoin and altcoins. In English social media circles, there is talk of "whales" dumping on "retail" when it comes to tokens and altcoins. In Mandarin, there's talk of "jiu cai" or chives as the embodiment of a naive retail investor who is promised a ton of return on cryptocurrencies—while the rich "whales" in the shadows get to sell tokens without investor protections.

Yet beyond the financial return, people work on censorship-resistant communication platforms, and Bitcoin miners speak of their fascination with money without the state. It's hard to get a very clear read of exactly what kind of sentiment exists about Bitcoin as the topic is more censored. Chinese Internet users have flocked to Nostr and decentralized communication apps built on top of it like Damus. On a podcast episode of "Tom and Jerry Discover Bitcoin," one Chinese Nostr user commented on how they thought there was only maybe "ten or so" content creators that thought about Bitcoin outside of its price in the Mandarin-language ecosystem. They resorted to going to English documents and translating them back into Mandarin in order to access thinking beyond technical analysis. But with the creation of Nostr, a censorship-resistant relay of information, and apps like Damus that act as clients to facilitate cross-border communications, he found that the Chinese Bitcoin community finally had a place to discuss issues beyond the price.

The most popular Mandarin-language podcast on Bitcoin, one that features a Bitcoin maximalist view, is actually hosted in Malaysia. "Tom and Jerry Discover Bitcoin" features conversations with many Mandarin-language speakers and features episodes mostly in Mandarin. The fact that the most prominent Mandarin-language podcast in the world on Bitcoin is in Malaysia and not the People's Republic of China is a testament to what a hot-button and censored topic Bitcoin has become in China. The podcast features interviews with many Bitcoiners who have connections to China and is conducted in Mandarin, though often with a mix of English depending on the speaker in question. As an example, Samson Mow has come onto the show to discuss his role as a "small blocker," somebody who wanted to keep Bitcoin's block size constant in the blocksize war. There are also discussions with many builders in the Bitcoin space and (given the popularity of Nostr in Asia) adjacent "freedom technology tools." Nostr uses a Bitcoin-like approach except that it replaces nodes with relays—people transmit messages with one another. It tends to cluster many Chinese Bitcoin community leaders, though Nostr has a following all of its own—with the attractive ability to separate your online identity from your real identity (a difficult task in China that is becoming more difficult with the need to register "real ID" for access to virtual platforms).

Table 1: Sample Bitcoin-related Nostr accounts

Nostr Accounts	NPub Key	Description
sherry	npub1ejxswthae3nklj avznmv66p9ahp4wm j4adux525htmsrff4qy m9sz2t3tv	A local organizer and coder who is building the Hong Kong Nostr community.
aLE	npub1pjvvr9we639fn 6kp9aqnf4rua5suwe8 mdvfygr0gegadhuxrw wnsz5jf67	Posts in Mandarin, adamant about the fact that Nostr is not Web3 and that Bitcoin is the future of currency, while Nostr is the future of communication.
BTCDiscovery	npub1uuluslh24d0clk 2j5e9lfrqncqzw2cgnta kkc5sat8pmtjtrhqhqn 6fxy3	The Nostr account associated with the "Tom and Jerry Discover Bitcoin Podcast."

An interesting proxy for interest in Bitcoin beyond discussions like this, especially in technical communities, is the number of repositories on Github, a shared codebase tool that allows people to collaborate and edit code or markdown documents that can serve as the basis of decentralized documents. There are about 550 repositories related to the Mandarin spelling of Bitcoin as of January 2024.[25] Those include a Mandarin translation of the original Bitcoin whitepaper and multiple books and tools related to the Bitcoin ecosystem—showing an intense interest in technical communities to learn more about Bitcoin. Chinese software developers will often use Github as a resource to consult and as a portal to the global Internet and open-source technology stack—and it's not something the Chinese party-state has been able to ban because of how critical Github code is.

How the Chinese Internet thinks and discusses Bitcoin is mediated by the Chinese party-state and its tight censorship and hold on the Chinese Internet. Diaspora communities or those using VPNs within China have relatively free rein to discuss what they want. However, those who use the Chinese Internet face restrictions. Even mentioning Bitcoin on WeChat can get one's account banned. As such, it can be very difficult to find the truth of what the Chinese Internet thinks about Bitcoin since the record of those discussions can be erased, and people can self-censor when they talk about topics the party-state doesn't favor. Though it's clear that Bitcoin isn't a topic that has been memory-holed like others, discussion of the topic can still be guarded—especially as it relates to the Chinese party-state's fears around central policy objectives like capital controls and keeping Chinese money within its borders and its controls.

The contrast with the Chinese diaspora is therefore striking. It is one of the most vibrant forces in the world, both virtually and physically. There should be no surprise that in a diaspora that is so wide—in 2019 it is estimated to be more than 40 million people spread across the world[26]—there are a variety of different perspectives on Bitcoin. Some diaspora members are exiled because of their activity in the Bitcoin space, offering an interesting perspective on how sometimes it takes shedding one's nation-state identity to join new digital movements. Other diaspora members champion the decentralization element of Bitcoin (and it must be said, other cryptocurrencies) because of their experience dealing with the repressive Chinese party-state. There are many who are silent either way on the topic. And there are some that are opposed to the Chinese party-state but also opposed to what they see as a "conservative" or "libertarian" movement. Yet Bitcoin has entered the conversation here. Wan Dang, one of the student leaders of the Tiananmen Square Movement, has solicited funds in cryptocurrencies for the cause, with his non-for-profit based on commemorating the events at Tiananmen Square accepting payments through Coinbase. The student leaders in exile have often faced a mixed reality with centralized services: famously, a senior executive at Zoom was indicted by the Department of Justice for censoring events on Zoom (allegedly at the behest of the Chinese party-state). There's an appeal to Bitcoin and decentralized ideas in general among those who have suffered perhaps the most at the hands of an all-powerful party-state that hasn't stopped its reach at its border.

Bitcoin Schools of Thought in China

One of th^e things to understand about Bitcoin is how certain Bitcoin supporters and developers regard Bitcoin as distinct from other cryptocurrencies. There are a few schools of thought in Bitcoin land: Bitcoin-only, Bitcoin-leaning, and Bitcoin-as-bridge.

For example, when I interviewed Louis Liu, the founder of Mimesis Capital, a family office dedicated to Bitcoin-only investment, I heard the word "shitcoin" so many times I lost count. This isn't surprising, given how Bitcoin-only people are derided as "maximalists" by other schools of thought. Traditionally, there's an age divide as well, with younger entrepreneurs in the Web 3.0 space inclined to treat Bitcoiners like "dinosaurs." However, Bitcoin-only people are the most in-tune with the ideological elements of Bitcoin, and probably the least among all groups to be purely profit-oriented.

Bitcoin-leaners tend to look at "altcoins" with skepticism but aren't fully bought into Bitcoin as the sole valid chain. They mostly cluster around Ethereum as another valid network, with varying degrees of altcoin scrutiny and acceptance. The original Ethereum team largely came about because of *Bitcoin Magazine* and the search for ways to run more arbitrary code on the chain and build new applications.

"Bitcoin-as-bridge" believers tend to view Bitcoin as obsolete. They may only accept Bitcoin in order to buy tokens from this project or another project, but mostly because most cryptocurrencies that aren't Bitcoin or Ethereum trade at low volumes, and it's difficult to get fiat on-ramps and off-ramps on them.

It's important to look at the stakeholders in the Bitcoin network and see where they might lean. Bitcoin is a set of game theory-based incentives. There are conferences and meetups, as well as personal relationships forged between different players in the space, but at the end of the day, Bitcoin relies on creating the right incentives for everyone across the board for its continued survival. For Bitcoin miners, their calculation is often a blunt one. How much cost do I need to take when it comes to energy in order to get Bitcoin that I can trade or hold? Bitcoin miners tend to be Bitcoin-leaners. The same infrastructure that allows them to store computing devices to mine Bitcoin can allow them to mine with other chains for which it is much less difficult—so many Bitcoin miners will also try their hand at mining Ethereum and perhaps other chains.

There are then investors, who buy Bitcoin and intend to hold it. These investors have gradually become more sophisticated and now include some of the largest institutional investors in the world—publicly traded companies like Tesla and famously MicroStrategy, and now even governments such as El Salvador. There's a huge variety of views here, but most people are focused on return, and so won't be Bitcoin-only. Institutional investors are unlikely to get involved at scale with altcoins other than the major coins because of their extreme volatility. Most will default to Bitcoin, but some will explore with Ethereum. Liu is strictly Bitcoin-only and one of the only family offices doing this, but he proclaimed that many people aren't as consistent, even among his inner circle.

There are also retail investors who form a large base of demand for Bitcoin and other tokens. The majority of money is in Bitcoin—a measure of Bitcoin's dominance—in part because Bitcoin has never had a lower "market value" than any other altcoin. These are the peers in Bitcoin's peer-to-peer network—the people using Bitcoin or holding it for profit. However, in the case of altcoins and new speculative tokens, they may sometimes be the victim.

The exchanges that most people use to retail Bitcoin and altcoins are another major player. They are incentivized to be prolific and sell as many tokens as people are willing to buy. This is why Binance offers so many trading pairs and why Coinbase sets out tokens it's trying to list. Some Bitcoin-only exchanges pride themselves on being Bitcoin-only, but they don't carry the vast majority of the traffic and demand for cryptocurrencies.

Finally, there are the coders, media, and community leaders, all of whom tend to be the most Bitcoin-only. Those who organize around Bitcoin-only have their own channels and large-scale companies built on scaling Bitcoin, such as Lightning Labs, which is focused on the Lightning Network layer two of Bitcoin—dedicated to reducing the cost of transaction fees and making Bitcoin more instant and easier to use. Bitcoin Core itself welcomes new contributors from any background.[27]

Bitcoin Culture in China

An important and maybe essential part of understanding Bitcoin's relationship with the People's Republic of China is Bitcoin's culture. After all, Bitcoin at the end of the day is a set of tools and network incentives bundled together along with many stakeholders. There are still people involved, and enough mass, given enough time, can change the underlying technology to meet their needs (for example, you can imagine a world where Satoshi's 21 million Bitcoin cap is modified). What ultimately ends up preventing that?

It's really the cultural aesthetic of Bitcoin and the people it gathers. Like any system involving humans, there is a balance between discretion and consensus. What binds Bitcoin together isn't just the technology: it's how the community onboards different people and engages with it and who joins as part of the system.

Bitcoin's culture therefore can be odd to describe, and it isn't uniform. Bitcoin picks up all sorts of people who might strongly disagree with each other on different topics: there are pitched debates on vaccines, diet, and everything else between Bitcoiners. Most Bitcoin adherents believe in less centralized control, especially state control. For Bitcoiners, their worst enemy is central bankers gone amok—but this skepticism toward authority extends to every tendril of the state. There are progressive Bitcoiners, and probably moderates on the spectrum that believe there is a role for government to play in Bitcoin. Just because you are a part of the system and its incentives doesn't mean you imbibe these values. Institutional investors and some miners are probably more motivated by the drive to get more fiat money out of the system: their cultural views on Bitcoin are not shaped by this discussion, and they may find it off-putting as they view Bitcoin as a small part of their money-making culture rather than a larger technological gateway to an array of more decentralized tools. Yet, as a whole, the system's effects tend toward eroding centralized authority and state power, and that attracts a certain crowd.

Some of the more common themes might have to do not with diet and politics, but a drive toward contention, upholding Bitcoin's "red lines" and conflicts with other chains. These debates extend into Mandarin-language spaces as well. On Clubhouse, which briefly bridged the Chinese Internet and the "free" global Internet, there were rooms that discussed NFTs and Ethereum and debated over whether or not to debate or add people who were "Bitcoin maxis." "Maximalist," meant as an epithet, has been embraced by Bitcoiners who see other cryptocurrencies as scams, and now has become a "red line" for some Bitcoiners. This is especially the case after several forks in Bitcoin led to a direct split in the chain and the creation of Bitcoin "clones" such as Bitcoin Cash. There are those that embrace some or many other cryptocurrencies and some of the developments happening on other chains including smart contracts, ICOs (initial coin offerings), DeFi (decentralized finance, wherein the promise of trading financial assets without an intermediary in the middle), NFTs (non-fungible tokens, which enforces scarcity for "ownership" of a digital asset, mostly used to designate ownership of digital tokens such as art pieces). Some Bitcoiners wholesale reject these applications and think of them as a trivialization of the "rightful" cause of Bitcoin and digital money: eroding the power of central banks and state authorities.

Others think these applications could be built on layers as part of Bitcoin or are a part of the Bitcoin ecosystem already. Those who feel strongly about this tend to refer to other tokens and cryptos as "shitcoins." Bitcoiners will deride Ethereum for having had to "reset the chain" during the DAO hack, splitting off into "Ethereum Classic" and the new-fanged Ethereum. They point out that ETH 2.0 has promised proof-of-stake for a long time and hasn't delivered, and proof-of-stake is just the same concentration of wealth that led to the need for Bitcoin in the first place.

Ultimately, the one thing that might unite Bitcoiners is a fierce drive toward guarding their community and its tenets against critics and those they see sabotaging the technology and movement. They are a testament to the contrarian nature of many in the Bitcoin community and their dedication to protecting the technology of Bitcoin. Yet this thorny side doesn't come without its costs—as well as its own magnetic force pushing Bitcoin forward—the incredible price growth and wealth it has created.

Buying Bitcoin in China

Bitcoin was first the plaything of Internet hobbyists, worth a few dollars at best. Somebody spent 10,000 Bitcoin on two Papa John's pizzas, marking one of the first times Bitcoin was exchanged for a physical good. That amount in 2023 would be worth more than $250MM in USD. Then it became an institutional force for investment, with public companies and funds embracing Bitcoin. And in 2023, even nation-states embraced it, with El Salvador adopting Bitcoin as legal tender. Bitcoin's price is an important part of its culture, but it isn't everything—yet the key price points of Bitcoin help anchors its co-evolution with the Chinese party-state's techno-nationalist rise. The interest in buying Bitcoin comes with price interest for many Chinese investors.

It might surprise people to learn that Chinese people can still access and buy Bitcoin. Despite a round of news on how China is creating "bans," it's difficult to fully restrict Bitcoin, just like VPN usage. This has become more urgent as Chinese investors have sought to invest outside of the Chinese stock market and domestic shores.[28] Even though most exchanges are not accessible within mainland China, other trade methods exist. There are private Telegram groups and even WeChat groups where people can go and find sellers and buyers directly. A private Telegram group that hosts Bitcoiners will typically have a rich conversation history you can search through and even reviews for buyers and sellers. They can also meet in public places and send each other payments to release Bitcoin from one private key to another wallet.[29] In this arena, the role of Tether, a stablecoin, comes into play. Tether offers the option to hold your cryptocurrency in a dollar-denominated asset that won't fluctuate in value with the US dollar.

Before the bans, it was reported that Chinese high-net-worth individuals were able to convert large amounts of fiat wealth into Bitcoin. The story of Mr. Li in one interview traces his beginnings in Bitcoin through his financial advisor, who managed to get him to convert his fiat holdings from real estate into Bitcoin. A second story involves a Mrs. Zhang, who consulted an overseas consultancy in the British Virgin Islands to get access.[30] After the exchange ban and the prosecution of several prominent cryptocurrency figures, activity in Bitcoin purchases in China shifted both to stablecoins like Tether that are still legal to trade yuan for and over-the-counter groups where people send each other yuan and receive Bitcoin in return. Some formalized groups were created out of exchanges like Huobi, whose OTC desk surpassed $100MM in trading volume. Others were taken into private chats and increasingly into physical spaces as time went on—for example, QQ groups, Telegram groups, WeChat groups, and even local computer shops.[31] Liu Wei is a pseudonym of an owner of a

WeChat OTC trading group. He claimed that he was doing about 300,000 RMB in trading volume a day, and making a matching fee of between 0.5% to 1% for each trade from his activities, generating about 90k RMB of monthly revenue.[32]

Chinese buyers of Bitcoin now face a few different paths. They can communicate online or offline with sellers whether through apps or offline conversation. The seller would tell them how much yuan they're willing to take, and if a buyer chooses to go down this path, they have to send the yuan first and then wait for the Bitcoin later. This has created the need for trustworthy sellers. WeChat groups will (for example) often host reviews and a rich history of proven Bitcoin sales to reassure buyers. Buyers can also go through more formal OTC desks as well overseas, though those are being restricted more and more (for example, shops in Hong Kong are no longer as prominent as they once were). Or they can buy Tether using yuan on Bitcoin exchanges and then hold the Tether or exchange it further for Bitcoin.

It's clear that it's difficult to track a lot of the activity since most of it happens in grey-zone over-the-counter trading, where no ledgers are reported publicly in an accessible manner—which is part of the point. If there was an easy way to track this activity, the Chinese party-state would likely have gone after everybody involved. Hong Kong has often been a gateway to trade fiat for Bitcoin for mainlanders, especially after the mainland crackdown, but the Hong Kong government itself is trying to move activity from OTC trading desks to "regulated" and licensed exchanges.[33] In this role of bridge, stablecoins also play as important of a role as Hong Kong did. When China banned Bitcoin exchanges and trading yuan for Bitcoin, Tether, a stablecoin pegged to the US dollar 1:1, replaced the yuan for Bitcoin trades for Chinese exchanges. This change happened almost exactly in sync with the ban on Bitcoin exchanges, marking Tether as the probable on-exchange trading currency for Bitcoin from people who used to pay with the yuan.[34] This was no coincidence—Tether and the Bitfinex exchange are tightly linked. Paolo Ardoino, who is the CEO of Tether, as of early 2024 used to be the CTO of both Tether and Bitfinex.[35] Both teams share senior team members with each other and both Bitfinex and Tether are subsidiaries of iFinex, Inc. Bitfinex and Tether combined together to promote in China—for example, through Zhao Dong, the king of OTC (over-the-counter) cryptocurrency trading, who founded RenrenBit and was a minor share-holder in Bitfinex.[36] By activating Bitfinex's existing channels for reaching Chinese cryptocurrency investors, offering a stablecoin that wasn't banned as explicitly as a way to exchange against foreign currencies and cryptocurrencies, and shifting its business away from the United States, Tether and Bitfinex found a potent bridge to many Tether buyers, including some in China.

Tether as a Bitcoin Bridge in China

Capital controls and stablecoins can be at odds with one another. Stablecoins are digital assets allowing users to trade other cryptocurrencies without a fiat onramp or offramp. Reserves back them at a 1:1 ratio. For example, Tether, which stemmed from the Bitfinex exchange, backs the number of Tether bought with reserves in USD or other forms of short-term debt considered safe.[37] Stablecoins play an interesting role here, allowing people to transit money between different systems while preserving its value—sometimes in defiance of capital controls. In 2021, about half of Bitcoin traded against the stablecoin Tether.

This exchange allowed the owners of Tether's reserves to invest the created reserves, which they did in large amounts of commercial paper (among other things). This gap existed because banks did not know how to handle this new asset and by and large refused to get outside of their domestic moats to service an international financial tool that allowed for more seamless communication between different financial systems—either out of inability or fear. Tether has been expanding throughout the years, with more dollars in company reserves, at least on a nominal basis. Where that expansion has come from, as well as what investments that expansion is in, form a bridge between Bitcoin and China, another intersection point between Bitcoin and the People's Republic of China. Large volumes of commercial paper were added to the global economy by integrating China's companies into corporate debt. While there was speculation that the Evergrande debacle (a debt crisis among one of China's largest real estate companies) might have taken down Tether, the company behind it maintained that it did not hold any Evergrande paper.

When fellow stablecoin Terra fell apart, Tether stuck to its stated policy that it had a 1:1 reserves relationship with the amount of Tether issued—essentially saying that 100% of Tether was collateralized by purchasing the equivalent amount of fiat reserves.[38] However, some reserves, including the recent uptick in holding Bitcoin and some reserves in precious metals, are volatile. The majority of

Tether's reserves are cash and cash equivalents, of which most are placed in US Treasury bills. Tether uses Cantor Fitzgerald for custody of its US Treasury bills, which form the vast majority of the reserves Tether claims.[39] Any user should be able to trade every Tether token for its equivalent US dollar—unlike in fractional banking, where banks only hold a percentage of what is required to make all their deposit-holders whole.

Since it is permissionless, Tether is a way to enter the Bitcoin economy from fiat without relying on stringent regulations or getting your bank account frozen or shut down as happens with Chinese bank account holders. Since buying from cryptocurrency exchanges is banned and can get account numbers frozen, Chinese volume for Bitcoin mostly comes from over-the-counter exchanges where Chinese yuan is traded for Tether, which is then sent to various exchanges such as Binance that are still headquartered in jurisdictions like Southeast Asia. Tether demand in turn pumps up Bitcoin demand, as USDT to Bitcoin trade is more scantily regulated.

Tether has become more and more important as it becomes much more difficult for people to trade from RMB or Chinese digital payment rails to Bitcoin. As Chainalysis has demonstrated, Tether trading on Chinese exchanges exploded from the 4th quarter of 2017 to the 2nd quarter of 2019, going from 12% of global Tether trade to a whopping 63%. Tether has decided to invest some of its profits into Bitcoin itself.[40] As of May 2023, Tether had a market cap of about $82B, and represents a huge force in Bitcoin's growth. No matter the level of regulation, Chinese residents and citizens still seem willing to take the risk and buy Bitcoin or Tether—though in recent months, Tether has come under scrutiny as well, with SAFE (responsible for enforcing China's capital controls and foreign exchange) asking local officials to police Tether usage (one Chinese citizen was sentenced to nine months in prison for earning about $20 USD in commissions from selling USDT to another).[41]

What Is the Future of Bitcoin in China?

If this is the present and past of Bitcoin and China, what does the future look like? With the Lightning Network, Bitcoin is looking to become a medium of exchange, and flip people's perceptions of it being merely "digital gold" to looking more like a real-time, technologically enabled currency that can be used in daily life. This is the use case of Bitcoin that the Chinese party-state is most afraid of and has made explicitly illegal in order to try to discourage it. For customers used to the latency of credit card payments (basically near-instant), the Lightning Network doesn't fully work. Lightning offers a "layer-2" solution that allows for the opening of payment channels and nodes that offer people the immediate ability to transfer Bitcoin between different users. The hope is that Lightning Network will fulfill Bitcoin's ability to be a meaningful means of exchange, allowing for frequent and somewhat private transactions.

With the reduction of transaction fees, a more seamless payment network and micro-payments are now possible. This means that payments are now quicker, more secure, and more resilient. It opens the door to businesses using Bitcoin as a point-of-sale service and allows for the purchase of goods. Some Bitcoiners are already moving to a world where they store their Bitcoin in the most secure fashion possible—cold storage with hardware keys, while pushing their on-chain transactions to the Lightning Network in order to make rapid payments. This has the effect of both reducing transaction fees and on-layer costs, including energy costs. By settling transactions in a combined fashion, Lightning Network shows Bitcoin's ability to make fundamental innovations and get better at servicing user needs. With innovations like Taro and the ability to make multi-asset exchanges on the Lightning Network's map of nodes and continual innovation, the Lightning Network aims to boost the medium of exchange facet of Bitcoin to become a more viable currency worldwide.

Bitcoin used to stand alone. Now it's increasingly showing up on the balance sheet of public companies, becoming part of financial portfolios for institutional funds, and garnering the attention of nation-states (including both the United States and China). This has led to a situation where nation-states are seriously considering central bank digital currencies to shore up their currencies' digital adoption. While China's digital yuan is often cited, there have been other pilots worldwide. While the Federal Reserve hasn't (as of February 2024) indicated where they were going to weigh in on this, multiple studies have been conducted on the topic.[42] Central bank digital currencies are under consideration by most of the world's major central banks, and a majority of the IMF's member states are considering CBDCs, though only a few have worked their way to pilots.[43] As of February 2022, notable examples of countries that have piloted central bank digital currencies are Canada (Jasper), South Africa (Kahoka), Nigeria (digital e-naira), and Uruguay (e-peso). Many other states are in a proof of concept stage.

Yet rather than complementing Bitcoin, these currencies are what Bitcoin's vision is hedging against: central state control over trackable digital money. Early on, Bitcoin was best positioned to address the major economic power that was most aggressive about responding with a central bank digital currency: China. It isn't just central bank digital currencies that Bitcoiners are skeptical about. There is a deep suspicion among Bitcoiners, especially those who are more "maximalist," of other cryptocurrencies such as Ethereum or the wide variety of tokens and cryptocurrencies out there. This plays out in vivid debates between Ethereum proponents and Bitcoin proponents. Other cryptocurrencies try to attack Bitcoiners in multiple ways: for example, Ripple's CEO claimed that because Bitcoin relied on proof-of-work rather than proof-of-stake it was contributing to climate change.

Some Bitcoiners look at what has happened in the cryptocurrency "boom" and are trying to take some of its features for Bitcoin. Ethereum has a Turing-complete programming language and interpreter that allows for the creation of more advanced scripts and flows than the baseline primitives within Bitcoin. This has created the potential for non-fungible tokens—virtually signed assets that can have standing in physical and virtual spaces as "proof of ownership" over what might be replicable digital copies. Yet many look at the booms and busts of ICOs and the vaporware that has been created around token projects and argue that this is a bridge too far for Bitcoin, which above all else is a reliable and steady payment network. Still, there are others who support ordinals. Given China's NFT culture and adoption of NFTs in the Chinese Internet, it's likely that this (combined with Layer 2 payments and altcoins in general) will play a large role in China's future with Bitcoin—along with the increasing amount of wealth Bitcoin is building for the Chinese people.

Conclusion: Bitcoin's Wealth Creation

Bitcoin has grown larger as a technological, economic, and cultural force with its maturity and its price movement gathering the interest of a Chinese people now attuned to wealth through decades of state capitalism. This has meant that more and more people are aware of it, and strong institutional forces that might have been on the fence now have developed more entrenched positions. As Bitcoin grows in scope and size with each halving, and each growth in prices and community traction, the harder it becomes to ignore and the more it will be shaped by the culture around it—as well as provide a shaping mold itself.

In China, the association of wealth and technology has proven irresistible to many. The topic of wealth in China, after all, is everything. After a century of revolutionary turmoil, starvation, and cultural destruction, Deng Xiaoping normalized "getting rich as glorious." In many ways, a hyper-materialist culture has come to define Chinese society during the era of "socialism with Chinese characteristics." From an age of socialist struggle to an "age of ambition,"[44] a near-nihilistic pallor has descended upon Chinese society, dubbed the 精神空虚, or spiritual void—one that is only partially salved with the Forbes rich list or its equivalent. The Hurun Report is the Chinese equivalent of the Forbes 400. Among the 14 "blockchain entrepreneurs" featured in China's richest list in 2018 were a smattering of familiar names.[45] The founders of Bitcoin and cryptocurrency exchanges represented a large share of the wealth generated in the People's Republic of China, including Binance, OKCoin and Huobi. Bitcoin mining companies were also noted, with Bitmain co-founders and employees on the list as well. Most of the wealth related to Bitcoin was generated either by individuals holding it from early stages, those that created marketplaces that allowed retail investors access to Bitcoin and other altcoins, or the suppliers of Bitcoin mining equipment that came to dominate the world.

These newly created billionaires were always likely to draw the attention of a Chinese party-state that wants to rein in and control capitalism for its own goals. "Unbalanced" and speculative capitalism is a massive fear of the Chinese party-state, which would like capitalism within China (and outside of it) to serve the party's interests first. That some people can get rich off of this system is always a given, but they have to be careful not to step on the party's toes. Some of the "crypto" entrepreneurs are subsequently under house arrest or otherwise reined in by the power of the Chinese party-state—a process seen with Jack Ma and other traditional tech entrepreneurs as well.

After all, the Chinese party-state is keenly aware of how to mediate technology to bolster the party-state's power. The Great Firewall unleashes conversations that favor the party on Chinese social media while limiting foreign reach and influence to a few expats using more and more unsteady VPNs. While anyone on the Hurun Rich List would merit some scrutiny from party authorities, given that Bitcoin and cryptocurrencies are seen as speculative subjects that need to be censored by central authorities, the focus is even deeper on those who made their money from the sector. Chengpeng Zhao (CZ) is now in exile and under arrest by the American government—and will serve jail time- and Leon Li is now under house arrest. The Chinese party-state's focus on the area has ensured that any wealth generated from the subject is either reined in or crushed to the party's desires rather than the ambitions of the individual entrepreneurs who helped mature Bitcoin.

Chapter Three

The Chinese Entrepreneurs That Built Bitcoin

Many bright Chinese entrepreneurs have found themselves between Bitcoin and China in their fight for the future. The largest mining hardware providers are both Chinese companies: Bitmain and MicroBT. The mining pools aggregating the hash rate that secures Bitcoin were based in mainland China. Many of the world's largest and first Bitcoin exchanges also came to China, igniting an age where Bitcoin would become a more mature and sophisticated asset. The irony is that in the country with the most extensive techno-nationalist program in history, China's entrepreneurs would also be on the front lines building a stateless currency that could mollify and modify nation-states.

If there is a place where Bitcoin changed from hobbyists on laptops to a saleable product for global financial markets, it is in China. The entrepreneurs that would contribute so much to Bitcoin's ecosystem would all have different incentives and stories, but what united them was their active belief in the network and its incentives despite the disapproval of the Chinese party-state. Chinese entrepreneurs built many of the critical companies and organizations that pushed Bitcoin from a gangly teenager to a mature financial product. From mining hardware providers and mining pools to exchanges, individual Chinese citizens took bold bets on a technology that would soon fall under the Chinese Communist Party's scrutiny.

The Dawn of Mining and Mining Pools in China

Bitcoin mining seems complicated, but the reality is that it relies on a simple formula. Plug in a machine, focus its efforts on solving Bitcoin's algorithm, and sell the block rewards if the machine successfully mines a block. If more Bitcoin comes in than maintenance and energy costs go out, then that is a scalable Bitcoin mining operation. It is a matter of machines multiplied by energy multiplied by space. China had the capacity and human experience to build these specialized machines, with the smartest hardware manufacturing happening in Shenzhen and other top Chinese cities. The space and energy could be found throughout the different provinces of China, many of which could look to Bitcoin miners to generate economic activity amid stranded top-down energy projects, such as the hydroelectricity dams that dotted Sichuan province.

The first of these was ASICMINER, founded by an entrepreneur who went by the name Friedcat in 2012. He posted about the opportunity to invest in a budding company that would offer integrated circuits and specialized chips to mine Bitcoin on Bitcointalk, which was the preeminent hub in the world for Bitcoin matters by then. Friedcat claimed to represent the virtual identity of Bitfountain, which built ASIC devices that would allow for more efficient Bitcoin mining. His partners were his friends based in China, who had the hardware background needed to deal with the problems of these new chips, such as the excess heat they generate.

In March 2014, however, the project stopped paying out dividends.[46] The ASICMINER thread on Bitcointalk is now marked as being a potential scam. Users have joked throughout the years about their missing dividends and about the identity of Friedcat. The demise of ASICMINER, however, brought an unexpected result: some angry Chinese entrepreneurs lost money and would go on to create the Bitcoin mining companies that dominate the world today.

A Chinese firm, Canaan Creative, was one of the first to release a chip dedicated to mining Bitcoin around 2013. Unlike the previous generation of mining power, which stemmed from more general use cases, these were the first sets of chips designed from the ground up to optimize Bitcoin mining. These new chips were known as ASICs or application-specific integrated circuits. ASICs are more advanced hardware focused on squeezing out as much efficiency as possible for specific tasks. The average laptop has a CPU that performs most general tasks and a GPU that helps with graphics processing. For Bitcoin mining, companies have built chips that take up a minimum of space and fit in as much chip power as possible dedicated to the specifics of Bitcoin mining. Chinese entrepreneurs like N. G. Zhang, founder of the billion-dollar chip company Canaan, pioneered these chips.

Meanwhile, Chinese entrepreneurs who were decoding and reselling Nokia phones (a "grey" activity with legal concerns) needed GPUs to do it. So did owners of Internet cafes that existed to support China's growing video game culture. These "grey hat" technology areas helped foster technological innovation and the first wave of serious Bitcoin mining companies. Tellingly, the Chinese party-state has turned its back on gaming. Anti-addiction registries abound, and the government places restrictions on those who can play games, with specific periods reserved only for those under the age of 18. However, the needs of gamers helped foster a brand of technological innovation the Chinese state now terms wasteful—and which the rest of the world trades freely and derives value from.

MicroBT and Bitmain emerged soon after the development of ASICs. They created even more sophisticated chips, which has led to an evolution of speed and hardware dedicated to supporting and securing the Bitcoin network. This increased sophistication at the hardware layer led to an environment of increasing competition and the creation of social structures and Bitcoin mining pools dedicated to protecting the network.

Think of Bitcoin mining pools as a way of buying insurance for Bitcoin miners. One individual miner could be chugging along but due to sheer luck never get any return. The Bitcointalk thread that records the reason and rules for the mining pools specifically specifies how CPU owners could not mine anymore (e.g., spending "weeks" without finding any Bitcoin blocks mining with three separate CPU machines.). Pooling together and buying regular cash flow with access to many miners was seen as better.

Shixing Mao (known as Discus Fish) and Chun Wang, two Chinese nationals, founded f2pool in 2013, the first mining pool in China to reach scale.[47] There had been earlier attempts by the Chinese Bitcoin community to create a mining pool, but they had failed financially. At the time, ASICs such as the ones built by Canaan Creative were still regarded skeptically versus GPUs. But soon the amount of hashrate dedicated to the Bitcoin network would explode with both the advent of ASICs and new mining pools—auguring an age where Chinese entrepreneurs would build both the specialized mining devices needed to competitively mine for Bitcoin and the software needed to derive value from those devices meaningfully. By 2014, f2pool was a significant part of the Bitcoin mining ecosystem, taking up almost one-third of all hash power in the system.[48]

Shixing Mao started publishing some of the first Mandarin source documents and guides on Bitcoin mining after reading the Bitcoin whitepaper, an event he has described as perspective-changing. Bitcoin was not very well understood in China, but years before it became a global financial asset, Chinese entrepreneurs like Discus Fish were translating source documents into Mandarin, carving out mining guides, and getting involved in mining themselves. But f2pool and GPUs were only the beginning. Antpool was soon established after the founding of Bitmain, mirroring new specialized mining hardware and mining pools' software and social organization. As of July 2022, Antpool and f2pool were still the second and third-largest mining pools in the world in terms of Bitcoin hash rate, and the legacy they both left ensured that Bitcoin mining would evolve from the exclusive purview of solo miners into an enterprise in and of itself.

This concentration of mining hardware and the origin of Bitcoin mining pools became a point of contention within the Bitcoin community. Since then, Bitcoin has been dogged every once in a while by the idea that mining is more centralized than the network's ideals. After all, if mining pools can control large amounts of hash power, couldn't they marshal the force to attack the network instead of securing it?

F2pool and Antpool grew for eight years, providing large amounts of hash power to discover blocks and secure the Bitcoin network. They were significant players in many of the most prominent debates in the Bitcoin community, from Bitcoin vs. Bitcoin Cash to various fork and improvement proposals, and were criticized by some (including Ripple's CEO) for leading to a "Chinese" takeover of Bitcoin mining. However, this kind of accusation betrayed a simple inflammatory view of the topic and the history of Bitcoin mining's development in the People's Republic of China: a history that combined hardware/software entrepreneurs before the Chinese government knew to take a position on the topic, and a community of semi-exiles who were rewarded financially but sometimes punished politically for their affiliation with Bitcoin.

The Chinese mining pools were collectives with rules but were not by themselves the dominating forces or coordinated forces some critics described them as being. They were a large part of Bitcoin's development, but eventually lost some of the critical battles that came to define Bitcoin. However, the legacy of Chinese entrepreneurs in helping

Bitcoin grow from an infant to a teenager ready to take on the world lives on.

Discus Fish himself is now focused on the DeFi space and has deviated away from any form of Bitcoin maximalism. He founded a custodial wallet, Cobo Wallet, which focuses on many tokens. A "Bitcoin maxi" these days is liable to call him a "shitcoiner" above everything else, showing how the Bitcoin community has evolved. Jihan Wu, who co-founded Bitmain, now lives in Singapore. His dispute with his co-founder caused a split in the company—one that now mainly hosts its Bitcoin mining operations in the United States.[49] His co-founder Micree Zhan is likely still in Beijing—his few posts feature commentary on Bitcoin bans in the future. Wu went from being a financial analyst at a private equity firm to a rabid Bitcoin fan to a cryptocurrency provider. He founded 巴比特 (Babite), China's first community site focused on Bitcoin and is currently the founder of Matrixport, a financial services platform for cryptocurrencies. And N.G. Zhang went from studying to become a doctor to being part of Bitcoin's growth story and presiding over a publicly traded NASDAQ company.

These examples symbolize the "Chinese Dream" that the Chinese party-state trumpets and a complex relationship between Bitcoins, altcoins, and the profit motive. However, many of these entrepreneurs would eventually scatter to the winds despite playing a significant role in Bitcoin's growth—some exiled for the sin of being Chinese and interested in a technological tool the Chinese government would struggle to understand, while not playing by the rules set by the same party-state: some wise rules, but also some that were overly restrictive.

The Rise of Bitcoin Exchanges in China

Bitcoin mining helps secure the Bitcoin network and attribute credit to "discovered blocks." It helps move block rewards to people, dedicating computing power toward securing the distributed data store that Bitcoin is. However, how are those Bitcoins traded with buyers once mined and made available?

Exchanges play a vital and evolving role in the Bitcoin ecosystem. Very few people have access to Bitcoin miners these days—the hardware is super-specialized and expensive. As a result, most Bitcoin holders will have bought their Bitcoin on an exchange. But exchanges are a double-edged sword for Bitcoin's growth. They offer convenience in return for increased risk.

At its core, Bitcoin is a set of private and public keys that prove that a user owns a certain amount of Bitcoin. With a private key and the right software or hardware wallet, any user can send funds anywhere in the world within a few minutes by simply matching their private key with the public key to which they want to send funds. One of the tenets of Bitcoin is that it is censorship-proof and that self-custody is possible. Many individuals with standard bank accounts have banking limits on how much money they can withdraw or send to others. If users use Bitcoin as intended, they can avoid this problem.

Exchanges deal with two problems for most people: providing a simple user interface for holding funds and the "private keys" required and the ability to trade fiat money such as your US dollar or yuan for cryptocurrencies. In return for these two value props, an exchange has to take over custody, acting as a bank-like entity. They have a unique role in Bitcoin's growth, providing the gateway for most people to access and buy Bitcoin and creating the conditions for explosive growth. But that comes at the cost of most people trusting their Bitcoin with new actors, some of whom have proven to be unscrupulous and losing user funds—or stealing them. In the heady days of Bitcoin's ascent, Chinese entrepreneurs played a considerable role in creating the exchanges that would eventually power most of the world's trade in Bitcoin.

BTCC, Huobi, and OKCoin: The First Generation

In the earliest days of Bitcoin, most of the activity was in English-language forums and trade channels. Then, as with mining pools, Bitcoin entrepreneurs set out to build exchanges after being part of the Bitcoin community and learning more about it. Many of the early members of the Chinese Bitcoin community (and it was tiny at the time) would go on to create businesses that scaled to billions of dollars in market capitalization. However, it started with small poker rooms and speeches where nobody in the hall had ever heard about Bitcoin—even among the Chinese tech elite.

BTCC, the first Chinese Bitcoin exchange, was originally just a two-person team of Linke Yang and Xiaoyu Huang maintaining a website. It was trading a few hundred Bitcoins a day back when Bitcoins were barely worth anything in fiat terms. Helping BTCC connect with the Chinese banking system and helping it scale was Bobby Lee's contribution to elevating the exchange.

Lee had gotten into Bitcoin through his brother, Charlie Lee, who founded the first significant altcoin: Litecoin. He was raised in the United States and worked in the Chinese tech sector. His interest started with mining as a hobby. In a poker game hosted mainly for Chinese VC and tech figures, he would spread the word relentlessly. One of the games introduced Chengpeng Zhao (CZ), Binance's founder, to Bitcoin. Eventually, Lee would shut down his first mining stint, but only after getting a taste of Bitcoin and becoming an advocate.

In this relatively new era for Bitcoin, the party-state did not have a strong opinion, and mainstream Chinese tech companies started championing Bitcoin. Baidu, for example, was one of the Chinese tech titans that embraced Bitcoin for online payments back when it was worth just USD 200.[50] Lee described betting 10 BTC on the result of Super Bowl XLVII in 2013. His cherished 49ers lost, meaning he would lose a few hundred dollars (in 2023, that bet would be worth more than $300,000).

At this time, interest in Bitcoin would snowball, and so would its price. In 2013, the first spike occurred, where Bitcoin surged to USD 1,000. The early days of ignorance were soon replaced by more excitement, awareness, and demand for Bitcoin in China. The largest exchange in the world at the time was Mt. Gox, which was based in Japan. However, Mt. Gox was not accessible to people in mainland China and did not accept yuan in return for Bitcoin. This currency gap was an issue for most Chinese investors since there was and continues to be a yearly limit on the amount of foreign currency that can be exchanged for yuan each year. BTCC had to scale quickly to deal with the demand from Chinese buyers holding yuan, taking on institutional venture capital and hiring people at scale. Lee attempted (and was successful) at recruiting a slew of Bitcoin OGs like Samson Mow and even CZ (before the latter ultimately decided to become the CTO of another exchange).

Other competitors would quickly emerge to fill in this demand as well. Huobi and OKCoin were founded around this time. (Leon Li) founded Huobi; it represented another merger of the business and academic elite in the PRC with the rising new Bitcoin movement. Li was an alumnus of Tsinghua University's computer science program. Tsinghua is one of China and Asia's top universities, with a notable record of graduating engineering and scientific leaders. After working for Oracle, he decided to build a Bitcoin exchange. On August 1st, 2013, Huobi launched a simulated trading game, and then an actual Bitcoin exchange was launched a month later. Huobi would raise money from venture capital funds with a deep background in China, notably Sequoia Capital. With a $10 million war chest from Sequoia and funds from angel investors, Huobi was poised to grab momentum and seize the Bitcoin trading space in China. By December 2013, it surpassed BTCC and became China's largest Bitcoin exchange by trading volume.

But Huobi also started to get into trouble around the time it outgrew BTCC. Once it has established its brand and reputation as China's top exchange, the regulatory environment around Huobi would change dramatically from curiosity to outright hostility. Actions on the company's part did not help: excess funds were at one point invested into wealth-management funds, and different Bitcoin and Litecoin amounts were deposited into the wrong accounts.[51]

Okcoin was another Chinese exchange founded in 2013 by a figure who crossed over from the conventional Chinese technology ecosystem. Star Xu had several technical roles at leading tech companies in China, from Yahoo's China division to Alibaba. Okcoin, like Huobi, derived funding from venture capitalists, including a slew from the People's Republic of China. Like Huobi, it also rose rapidly before having to suspend trading at multiple points, with one notable time being the 2013 People's Bank of China (PBoC) notice and the other being the 2017 exchanges ban. Today it operates a US-compliant OKCoin money transmitter that allows purchasing cryptocurrencies from certain states but does not service any clients within mainland China.

The Chinese party-state issued a regulatory notice in 2013, warning exchange owners and the broader Bitcoin community that there was a new awareness of Bitcoin among Chinese tech elites and at the higher echelons of party-state regulation. The Chinese party-state forbade Chinese banks from interacting with Bitcoin. It was the first warning shot of many as China's political leadership wrestled with what to do with this brand-new technology.

Binance: The Second Generation

Between 2013 and 2017, there was wild price action and increasing demand for Bitcoin worldwide, both trends that benefited Chinese exchanges immensely. Then the creation of altcoins helped accelerate their growth even further and set the stage for the second generation of Bitcoin exchanges in China. Exchanges took on a new scale and scope with the emergence of Ethereum's ERC-20 standard, allowing exchanges to grow exponentially with new offerings. ERC-20 permitted almost anybody to create a token easily, beginning a wave of what was known as ICOs, or "initial coin offerings." Companies started approaching

ICOs as a new way to finance themselves: issue a controlled token pool and then sell those tokens to users in quasi-unregulated secondary markets.

The advent of so many different tokens also offered an immense opportunity for exchanges, which could benefit from listing and transaction fees from anybody looking to buy. One of these exchanges, Binance, was created to take full advantage of this. Its founder, CZ, has become one of the most prominent figures in the Bitcoin space. His story followed a typical one for the Chinese diaspora. The Chinese party-state exiled his father to the rural area of Jiangsu for being a counterrevolutionary and an intellectual. This period of exile happened shortly after CZ was born, while China was still in the throes of unwinding the Cultural Revolution when Maoist-era Red Guards called and punished intellectuals as the "臭老九" or the "stinking old ninth"—an old historical legacy of the Mongol-led yuan Dynasty that classified intellectuals and thinkers as the second-lowest caste in China (above only beggars).

As a result, CZ moved with his family at the young age of twelve to Vancouver, Canada, did his university studies in computer science at McGill University in computer science, and since then has regarded himself as a "global citizen" (世界公民). The term is fraught with meaning given China's recent history of expelling its citizens and the immense reach and depth of the Chinese diaspora worldwide.

CZ's career followed a windy path from working on Blockchain.info with Roger Ver to being the CTO of OKCoin and founding his exchange, Binance. Binance itself has grown furiously since the June 24th, 2017, ICO that led to its creation with the release of Binance Coin (BNB). In July

2022 became the world's largest exchange when measured by trading volume.

An essential part of Binance's growth has been offering the ability to add leverage to digital cryptocurrency trades and trade on their derivatives. It has also started with not dealing with fiat on-ramps and off-ramps, which usually triggers heavy regulations, meaning that the business model always gravitated to lower regulation and crypto-for-crypto trades. The leading competitor at the time, Bittrex, was facing technical issues and could not serve the vast number of new users trying to get onto the platform. At one point, it suspended new account registration. With lower fees and an ever-increasing amount of features, Binance soon leapfrogged over Bittrex. However, this growth came with rough bumps, especially given the Chinese party-state's increasing hostility toward cryptocurrency trading.

CZ initially registered Binance in China in 2017. As a result of increasing regulations as well as the pressure the Chinese party-state put on cryptocurrencies, CZ moved Binance's servers from mainland China to Hong Kong. Many exchanges based in mainland China were forced to shut down during the move—yet it was CZ's quick thinking and the gravitation to Hong Kong (which had not yet folded into the Chinese system and still maintained some veneer of "one country, two systems" independence) that helped save and preserve Binance's growth.

Binance and other exchanges have attracted the ire of the Bitcoin community at large. Exchanges are incentivized to make money by collecting as many fees as possible and have sold many tokens, including their own exchange coins. The Securities and Exchange Commission (SEC) lawsuit against Binance for selling its own BNB token and other securities laws, among other things, comes as no surprise.[52]

The Chinese party-state forced BTCC to shut down in 2018, unwinding its assets. Lee is proud that they could compensate employees and everyone who held funds in the exchange. Huobi's escape plan was to leave: first relocating to its Seoul office and then wandering around the world as a digital exile. Its source of financing became a listing on the Hong Kong Stock Exchange after a reverse takeover of an electronics company. However, by September 2021, Huobi had declared that it would no longer serve any clients from mainland China due to the regulatory stance of the Chinese party-state. A Bitcoin company that had started its roots in mainland China had gradually become one that served the rest of the world everywhere except where it began.

Even as the first generation of Chinese Bitcoin exchanges gradually receded, Binance continued to grow, serving more and more people worldwide as the team bounced from location to location, fulfilling CZ's vision of "global citizenship." Binance, founded by a Chinese Canadian tech entrepreneur who was first forced to leave the country because of the Cultural Revolution, then forced to leave the country a second time because of cryptocurrency regulations, is a reminder that those who are ethnically Chinese may sometimes be at odds and ends with the Chinese party-state's views. The conflict between the Chinese party-state has left some of the most prominent members of the (ethnically) Chinese Bitcoin and cryptocurrency community in exile. So it is with CZ, who, as of 2022, had resided in Singapore before his arrest by American authorities.

FTX: The Third Generation
and the Lessons of Exchanges

FTX is yet another story of a cryptocurrency exchange that left a region with ties to China after "sunny" cryptocurrency regulations got too hot. Starting in Hong Kong, the company has moved its headquarters to the Bahamas. A separate exchange, FTX.US, makes cryptocurrencies available for American residents. It has not only gotten notice because of its aggressive growth trajectory but also because of the notable brand partnerships and sponsorships it has embarked on—everything from sponsoring chess tournaments to buying the naming rights to the Miami Heat's stadium. Founded in 2019, FTX saw a rapid rise into the world's top cryptocurrency exchanges. It took the Chinese route of raising venture capital to another extreme with a $18 billion valuation and raising $900 million in capital from tech funding stalwarts such as Sequoia and Softbank. In 2022, it was engaging in an aggressive buyout of different crypto funds and services, further expanding its reach by using its well-capitalized position to sweep up rivals or complementary services that were not careful with their financial discipline in looser times.

FTX crossed paths with the Hong Kong cryptocurrency scene, with physical and OTC exchanges being part of the story of FTX's initial founding. However, today it is perhaps best known for its fall, with its discredited founder SBF becoming a household name for "failed boy genius," investing client funds without their consent and being indicted by the Department of Justice—and ultimately sentenced to 25 years in prison. By taking funds from clients and using them to prop up Alameda, its trading fund, FTX opened itself up to fraud charges. For those who believe in self-custody as the Bitcoin way, FTX was just another greedy exchange in selling and listing different tokens. While Binance is still alive and kicking in late 2023, FTX has met its demise.

There are a few things that unite the Bitcoin exchanges from all generations. Chinese tech founders working in traditional technology companies created most of the centralized Bitcoin exchanges in China. They raised rounds of financing from venture capitalists interested in getting involved in Bitcoin in a way that allowed them to bank traditional profits more akin to familiar Internet businesses. The first wave of entrepreneurs who popularized and established Bitcoin exchanges were not ideologues per se. However, people wanted to apply their knowledge and experience scaling tech products to a new monetary system. From that, they drew on experience with China's growing tech sector and either raised financing through the traditional VC funding route or, in the case of Binance, an initial coin offering.

Many of the Bitcoin exchanges in China started early. Bitcoin China (BTCC) was founded in 2011 and claimed it is the "world's first Bitcoin exchange." As more and more altcoins were added to the world, from upstart Ethereum to Litecoin, the exchanges morphed from Bitcoin services toward a more holistic sale of different altcoins and Bitcoin. Some chose to specialize more in Bitcoin-altcoin and altcoin-altcoin trades rather than focusing on Bitcoin-only or the trade of Bitcoin for fiat currencies of different kinds and others started offering derivatives products and ways to bet on cryptocurrencies with leverage. This drive toward altcoins made sense from an incentives perspective. Exchanges, after all, make money on fees for the amount of trading volume that goes through them. Unless there is a robust and principled reason (like opposition to ICOs and the consequences for certain retail investors), exchanges would want to allow altcoins that people want to buy and sell to profit from the trading fees and trading demand—otherwise other exchanges would win. Some exchanges trumpet that they are Bitcoin-only, yet this is not a trend frequently seen in China. Since many of the centralized Bitcoin exchanges in China have become the largest in the world, this had an outsize effect on how altcoins, Bitcoin, and fiat currencies became traded not just in China but worldwide.

How exchanges started, competing with one another over user fees, has today turned into a global arms race where exchanges with Chinese or Hong Kong roots offer the full gamut of altcoin, derivatives, leverage, and margin to entice new users. Not only does it make sense to offer altcoins, but it also makes sense to offer leverage, derivatives, and other ways of making bets on the prices of cryptocurrencies. Most Bitcoin exchanges in China compete against one another with features like this and have learned from this initial period what to do regarding global competition. Binance, for example, went from being an exchange that could be viewed as having Chinese roots to now a truly global exchange and venture, with subsidiaries geographically dispersed worldwide.

The idea of self-custody (where you have your keys and access to your own Bitcoin) and the reality of having much of the world's Bitcoin supply and accessibility held in the same sort of banking system as Bitcoin is trying to erode is an irony that is not lost on most people. There are decentralized and local exchanges where people can physically meet other people to transact in Bitcoin and ways to access Bitcoin mining operations and purchase Bitcoin wholesale. Solutions like Fedimint aim to bring custody back into the hands of Bitcoin holders rather than to the equivalent of corporate banks for Bitcoin. Nevertheless, most people buy and sell Bitcoin and other altcoins in ways the Chinese market helped accelerate.

Throughout the wave of regulations on Bitcoin and cryptocurrency exchanges, many centralized Bitcoin exchanges that started in China have, at various times, suspended services and access to user funds for Chinese clients—which would be a perfect use case for the decentralized exchanges and local exchanges built upon more censorship-resistant peer-to-peer trade. However, in practice, these solutions have yet to take on the scale that centralized exchanges have. But this may change soon after the experience of companies such as FTX that have criminally misused user funds.

An exchange like Paxful, for example, aims to maximize the number of ways somebody can buy and sell Bitcoin. In theory, somebody can directly offer their Bitcoin for cash or gift cards, which might be a way for enterprising PRC residents or citizens to get their hands on Bitcoin. Since this is less of an exchange than a listing site, Paxful can technically operate in the PRC. However, while there are plenty of offers, the trading volume pales compared to the centralized exchanges that have the world's largest trading volume. Most people will trade on over-the-counter trading desks where people offer Tether for RMB, and then people are free to buy other altcoins and other investment options on any exchange.

Conclusion: Bitcoin VCs and Investors

A relatively recent addition to the Bitcoin community has been the creation of venture funds dedicated to supporting Bitcoin startups. While many of the Bitcoin exchanges in China grew due to traditional venture capital support, a new breed of VC is now dedicated to Bitcoin. Surprisingly, despite government crackdowns, VCs of this type inevitably have a link to China—and some are based there.

In the early days of Bitcoin, investors of all stripes were barely aware of Bitcoin. However, those days are long past. Now, cryptocurrencies and Bitcoin are on the radar of every type of investor, from Bitcoin-only family offices to retail investors. Most investors in East Asia focus excessively on return versus the underlying technology. For example, Louis Liu runs Mimesis Capital, a Bitcoin-only family fund based in Taiwan. His thesis is Bitcoin-oriented, and his investments include Swan Bitcoin, which helps with dollar cost averaging investment into Bitcoin-only—a method that systematically stacks and buys Bitcoin regardless of market conditions. However, he quickly admits that he stands alone even in his inner circle. Most people are trying to pull him into altcoins or tokens, with better "returns" promised. The recent rise in Ordinals and BRC-20 tokens on Bitcoin, Bitcoin versions of Ethereum NFTs and ERC-20 tokens, seems to have a lot of traction in Chinese communities. Mandarin speakers are a prominent part of the discussion, according to observers like Dovey Wan. Many BRC-20 tokens trade with a Tether pairing—the default replacement for yuan-to-bitcoin trade. Chinese investors today very much have a say in what direction Bitcoin will go.

Bitcoin's growth phase came out of China. Chinese entrepreneurs built many of the custom computing chips that help mine Bitcoin and keep the network secure and viable. They then built the exchanges where most people in the world now go to transact between fiat currency and Bitcoin. Finally, many Chinese investors bought Bitcoin on an individual or institutional basis to further push Bitcoin's growth. This all came about even though the government that ruled them would soon find reasons to worry about Bitcoin.

Chapter Four

Trouble at a Second Glance

Bitcoin and China make an odd couple. Chinese entrepreneurs and tech companies defied the party-state and helped make Bitcoin the force that it is now. At the beginning Bitcoin was obscure and not well-known, and generally seen as perhaps trivial. Bobby Lee remembers going to a talk where not a single Chinese tech member knew anything about Bitcoin. Soon, however, the fledging project would grow into a global force, thanks partly to the Chinese entrepreneurs who built mining companies, exchanges, and invested in the new asset. It was at this greater scale that the Chinese party-state recognized the threat that emanated from Bitcoin, especially over areas of primal concern for the Chinese Communist Party's interests: the flow of capital within China, the level of corruption, party control over the black and white cat that "socialism with Chinese characteristics" produced, and the environment and energy policy.

It was trouble at a second glance—and since this recognition has come about, China has been the largest world economy to pursue the quickest and most draconian restrictions on Bitcoin. The Chinese system has been set up to be particularly sensitive to the themes of Bitcoin, from the ability to transact with peers around the world without censorship to the environmental considerations behind different forms of computational power and proof-of-work mining. Perhaps its most sensitive consideration is the yuan and its fear that it might be displaced.

Hard vs. Soft Currency

The distinction between "hard" money and "soft" money is the difference between a currency backed with a commodity that is practical such as gold and silver, and the "paper" or virtual money that forms what is essentially the currency supply of today. For this, economic historians point to the Bretton Woods system built after WWII that guaranteed gold conversion for the most liquid trading currency of the time, the United States dollar. After Nixon broke this system in 1971 and let the United States dollar float independently of gold, he essentially created a world reserve currency that central banks could control and manipulate. Given how today the vast majority of "money" circulates as electronic bank reserves and not as the paper notes often recognized as money, currency has never been "softer" than before, without any true backing. During the Bretton Woods system, 35 US dollars were guaranteed to bring you back one troy ounce of gold: this was the central tenet of the system. But today you cannot get a hard commodity at a guaranteed price back for your currency, and no bank window will redeem it for a set amount of gold. As a result, gold floats freely, one of many goods and services you can purchase with your unbacked currency. As of 2022, gold is trading in the $1,700/$1,800 per ounce range—a 50-fold increase in the price of gold compared to the going rate just 50 years ago.

What has happened? Simply put, the money supply has expanded, resulting in the dollar becoming less valuable over time, and thus requiring more dollars to buy the same amount of gold from before. The M-system of measuring monetary supply is a perspective that looks from narrow to broad: you start with M0 and go to M3, with each larger number being a broader measure of the monetary supply. M0 includes the coins and bills in circulation that an ordinary person might think of when they think of cash and currency. M1 considers not only cash in circulation but checking/savings accounts in banks—anything that can be very quickly converted into cash. M2 is a slightly broader way to measure money, and adds to M1 "near-money" accounts such as savings accounts that can be easily converted into physical cash in circulation if needed. M3 is the broadest measure that includes certain types of deposit accounts that can become cash quite quickly, but usually aren't seen as a way for the average person to settle their day-to-day expenses. The effect on money supply has been exponential: for example, the M2 monetary supply has exploded almost a thousandfold since the 1960s.[53]

The People's Republic of China has its own role to play in this system. Using the United States dollar as a reference, the PRC has engineered a system where it prices its own yuan at a managed rate so as to promote the state of the economy it wishes to produce. For the longest time in US-China relations, this meant keeping the yuan artificially low in value by using the "soft" capacity of the arbitrary fiat behind currencies to flood the market with yuan, purchasing dollars and foreign assets. This allowed the manufacturing base within the People's Republic of China to grow, turning China into the "factory" of the world and cheapening exports so that other countries would buy Chinese goods. As a result, the Chinese state treasury has held large amounts of US-denominated assets and was a banker for American debt (we don't know exact amounts since the composition of China's foreign reserves are a closely guarded state secret). It has prolonged the lifecycle of the "softer" United States dollar by propping it up through its own form of demand and by providing cheap exported goods that keep inflation down. And its managed currency exchange rate shifted the central banking system toward a system that emulates the Federal Reserve in many respects. The yuan can be seen as a "soft" currency built on top of the foundation of another "soft" trading currency. Any movement in US-China relations (as seen in the trade wars) could lead to the Chinese party-state deciding on another peg between the yuan and the US dollar—and any domestic oscillations could lead to the release of more yuan and more banking reserves into the system as well as a form of monetary stimulus - as well as a lower-priced yuan, and more Chinese exports into the United States.

However, the Chinese central banking system does not have some of the nominal safeguards associated with central banks in most developed economies. Central banks usually pride themselves on some level of "political independence." Although in the United States leaders are appointed by politicians and are subjected to very similar policy pressures as they are (for example, the need to create and "stimulate" jobs), it also means that there are some guardrails. When President Trump suggested a negative interest-rate targeting regime, something the European Central Bank had started as a means to even further stimulate the economy and to build a faster pace of job creation, he wasn't able to get this past Jerome Powell and the board of directors of the Federal Reserve. Even though he had appointed Jerome Powell, he could not fire Jerome Powell without cause, and this wall prevented the transfer of direct orders to the Federal Reserve system from the executive branch of the United States government. No such wall divides Chinese policymakers. The People's Bank of China, the Chinese central bank, reports and is subordinated to the State Council, the administrative overseer of the Chinese party-state. The Chinese central bank is often deployed as a tool within China's larger "battle of systems" with developed Western economies. As a result, the yuan is manipulated and its supply determined by a series of Chinese party-state economic objectives. It is semi-pegged to the United States dollar—not a fully floating currency allowed to trade under market dynamics, but a currency set to maximize state objectives. In the case of the yuan, China's central bank holds the yuan downward to accelerate the growth of a primarily export-led growth model.

Bitcoin's response to this situation of soft currencies built on top of soft currencies is a "harder" currency with a managed supply that doesn't budge according to the will and arbitrary whim of politicians for one nation-state. There will likely only ever be 21 million Bitcoins—it is a central tenet of the Bitcoin network. It would be hard to manipulate this rule: it is set at nearly a constitutional level rather than as a technocrat-level choice. But unlike a resource like gold, it doesn't rely on an exterior resource wherein the supply rate can be arbitrarily increased to meet fiscalized demand. This has political implications, and geopolitical ones as well, especially with the advent of countries that are relying on Bitcoin as a standard rather than other reserve currencies. Bitcoin offers the opportunity for individuals, institutions, and increasingly certain nation-states to "escape" soft currencies that are directed or dictated far outside the halls of local relevancy—a central threat to China's thesis of growth through a managed "soft" currency, kept reined in by capital controls and restrictions on what the Chinese people can do with their own money.

Capital Controls

Bitcoin's rise contrasted with decades of Chinese economic development centered around the techno-nationalist premise that was to come. Yet two elements of the Chinese system that came with its growing integration fueled a path for Bitcoin's most vital points of conflict with the Chinese party-state. One was the capital controls required to keep the stage-managed elements of the Chinese economy within Chinese borders. The other was the corruption and control embedded in the financial stage management by the Chinese party-state. In between, the environment serves as an argument that hides between these two issues.

One of the features of the ascent of China's yuan and the integration of the Chinese economy into the global

American trade system has been the use of capital controls. It can be challenging to take large sums of money out of China for Chinese citizens, and it is almost impossible for foreign investors to buy domestic versions of shares in China. This capital control has been the case since the beginning of the economic reform stage, and it speaks to the fundamental tension for the party between using incoming dollars for its ultimate plans and the need for control of those same dollars within its system to preserve its rule when the average citizen owns them.

Chinese entrepreneurs are the double-edged sword the party wields. Mao-era rules prohibited wage earners from getting bonuses for performance. That was one of the very first things Deng's economic policies changed. The Chinese people, used to being assigned into different classes and playing off one another according to arbitrary narratives, could suddenly make money for their needs, and often on their own terms. However, the party has always been careful about trying to thread the needle between giving the Chinese people enough freedom to help the state grow and maintaining control and legitimacy throughout the years. This was a tension that was fought between different factions at Tiananmen Square and still exists today: enough freedom to create economic growth on behalf of the Chinese party-state, but not enough to replace it altogether.

The tradeoff was made explicit regarding capital controls placed on individual Chinese citizens. Similar to the *hukou* residency system, which forbade rural villagers from settling into vastly growing urban areas, the party-state decided that the best way to allow capitalism to work for the state was to offer Chinese entrepreneurs the ability to build projects and to work and earn their wages—yet to ensure through various methods that their capital would not circulate outside of the Chinese banking system, where the Chinese party-state can maintain control could be maintained on entrepreneurs and their earnings. The Chinese banking system would, in turn, provide the funds required to create state-guided funds to invest in different technologies—powering another private-public partnership in various fields, from quantum computing to biotechnology.

China's economic rise marks a unique counter-thesis in a world where more and more capital controls were eliminated between the 1970s and onwards. From 2013 to 2017, the Chinese party-state had the world's strictest set of capital controls (until gradually moderating in 2017 to the thirteenth most strict).[54]

Chinese capital controls act in two ways: a long-term view of capital inflows/outflows being at the service of the state and as a potential short-term tool to cushion macroeconomic trends in the PRC. The Chinese capital control is accelerated by the unique nature of the Chinese banking system, which provides loans to favored sectors or infrastructure programs.

This sector favoritism in the domestic economy causes a "search for yield"—more risk and potentially more reward by investing outside of China. It also represents a "shield" for Chinese citizens—namely, some will choose capital flight and get money out of the system if they believe there is policy instability in the PRC or if they are about to earn the disfavor of the Chinese Communist Party. With the ratcheting up of an "anti-corruption" drive that has descended, at times, into score-settling, the latter has never been more top-of-mind for so many. China has constructed an economy where foreign direct investment is highly encouraged but where capital flight and exiting the system for its citizens is tightly controlled. It has done this by wielding political and economic tools that have helped shape modern finance and economics.

There are two types of capital control a state can implement: direct/administrative and indirect or more market-driven. The first limits how much currency an individual can bring into and outside a state, and the second is a tax on foreign currency transactions. The first involves legal limits, and the second involves trying to move the market to discourage certain capital inflows or outflows. The marquee capital control and the one that affects the most people is a yearly direct limit of USD 50,000 for Chinese citizens looking to make foreign exchange transfers from the yuan to other currencies—a limit upped from 20,000 USD on February 1st, 2017, but a stringent capital control nevertheless. A government agency (the State Administration of Foreign Exchange) must approve anything above this amount through a manual approval letter.

Capital controls are an area where Bitcoin bumps straight into the Chinese party-state's objectives—and reflects the desires of some Chinese people. Unique among most of the world's population, the Chinese people face a situation where there is a ton of money to earn, but with a catch: it will likely need be spent within China. This area of control is where Chinese policymakers may feel the most acute threat from Bitcoin, which serves a critical function as a peer-to-peer network designed for people to transact across borders that the Chinese party-state does not control.

Before 1994, this situation was even more acute. Foreigners had to buy "foreign exchange certificates" that could only be exchanged for yuan at black markets. Even now, currency black markets exist to smooth out the rough spots in demand from a semi-pegged currency for domestic audiences. While technically illegal, the markets exist so that people can exceed the $50,000 limit on foreign currency buys and get access to better rates than what regulated banks will provide. They tend to respond more to market demand trends for foreign currencies, especially the US dollar.

These "yellow bulls" have existed throughout the yuan's ascent and the opening up of China's economy. They are part black market currency traders and part scalpers. Wherever the state puts limits, for example, on the number of available train tickets, yellow bulls fill the space. They go to the main train stations, hawking their tickets as scalpers. Many of them are pregnant women, whom Chinese law cannot go against quickly. They represent a need for a peer-to-peer network more responsive to peer demand than the top-down mandates of local governments or the Politburo.

Bobby Lee, the founder of one of China's first Bitcoin exchanges (BTCC), is not convinced that Bitcoin's demand or price is correlated with capital controls.[55] He points out plenty of "other ways" to get around China's capital controls exist. He is not wrong. Canadian banks, for example, were caught helping Chinese citizens evade Chinese capital controls through a practice known as "smurfing."[56]

Smurfing involves circumventing the $50,000 a year a person in foreign outflows by using friends, family, and even distant business associates. As long as different account holders set up accounts, the transfer of funds between the Chinese banking system and "friendly" bankers such as those in foreign banks can proceed. The money then typically gets deposited into local real estate markets. There are also other practices, from misrepresenting travel expenses to buying casino chips in Macau. Companies are also subject to restrictions on investment amounts—misreported bank loan data and export data can help disguise effective violations of the $50,000-a-year limit.

There was an estimated $4.6B in capital flight out of China using Bitcoin between 2011 and 2018. By tracing the "yuan" premium for buying Bitcoin, where Bitcoin was priced more expensively in yuan, the study's authors were able to trace people who sold at a loss on foreign exchanges as probably correlated with Chinese capital flight: the purchase of Bitcoin in domestic yuan, and shortly after, obtaining (often at a loss) foreign currency for those same Bitcoins.[57] Those willing to take a capital loss were assumed to be paying a fee for the ability to conduct cross-country trade with some amount of pseudonymity, especially between CNY and USD. The other alternative would be to practice cross-border arbitrage, assuming that Bitcoin demand is more expensive in certain currencies. Since the trades took a loss (on average around 2% of the transaction volume), the analysis assumed that this was not for profit but to move funds across borders.

One interesting finding was an association of Bitcoin wallets tied to black market activity and capital flight, with capital flight being a separate category. However, it is hard to draw anything extensively conclusive on the topic because tracking the intent behind Bitcoin's flow is incredibly difficult and grows more complex as time progresses. The database used was correlated to FBI seizures and to Silk Road activity, which was a marketplace for recreational drugs online. This analysis may need to map more cleanly to illegal activity in China, especially in the context of a country with many strict laws on recreational drugs.

Another finding was that by measuring "economic instability" in Chinese policymaking, you can trace out and measure greater correlated demand for crossing Bitcoin between exchanges to get more USD. The index is based on either SCMP or People's Daily news articles. Bitcoin may be correlated with some capital flight, but the amount measured was trivial in the grand scheme: less than $5 billion over seven years. To put this into perspective, misreported travel expenses have been estimated at $100B+ a year of capital flight despite the $50,000 a person a year rule. This smaller amount was admittedly during Bitcoin's immature phase—a period when a Bitcoin could retail for a couple of US dollars and before it became an institutional force and central banks were placed in the treasury of nation-states. In practical effect, the amount Bitcoin has butted heads with Chinese capital controls is relatively low.

However, in the philosophy that animated the battle, we can start to see the theme of conflict between Bitcoin and China, something the Chinese party-state figured out early enough in its response. Bitcoin intrigued many Chinese entrepreneurs who saw the opportunity for profit and a currency without a government, which allows people to regain control of their assets and lives. The Chinese party-state and other nation-states are looking to entrench their economic and political control over their tax bases and the citizens they "serve."

With bans, policy statements, and physical actions that result from legal limits, the Chinese party-state is aiming to mold the future by fine-tuning the tools in its control, building a techno-nationalist narrative that other nation-states want to organize around as well: the idea that middle-income and low-income nations can become rich and have enduring power for their political leaders through a combination of long-term autocracy and the slow embrace of capitalism, while keeping critical functions—including technological development—in the state's arms tightly.

Bitcoin was created by an unknown person and not a state. It was generated and supported by open-source software, with people operating parts of the network for principle or profit. This network was expanded worldwide without any political force to restrict people within the system. The Chinese party-state's need for political control and for the party to hold its hand on the market creates a unique intersection between Bitcoin and corruption.

Corruption

Corruption is a long-standing and central problem identified by the Chinese party-state as primal to its survival. The Central Commission for Discipline Inspection (CCDI) is responsible for much of this activity. A long-standing institution for the Chinese Communist Party as a control mechanism for the party itself, acting as a version of "Internal Affairs" in a police department, the CCDI has waxed and waned depending on China's political leadership. In the Mao years, the CCDI was often reformed into different organizations, and, at various points, the CCDI was even criticized or purged by Mao.

Since the end of the Cultural Revolution and the imposition of the Dengist system, the Politburo Standing Committee was so elevated in power that members were assumed to have criminal immunity, a norm broken in Xi Jinping's rule quite early. As Xi has highlighted the anti-corruption drive as central to his rule, many media sources have highlighted his direct involvement in CCDI actions. Xi's campaign has taken down "four Tigers," senior members of the Chinese Communist Party who were once seen as above criminal prosecution. It is also extended to many "flies"—a broader amount of prosecution of lower-level party members than previously seen. However, the "anti-corruption" campaign has sometimes been viewed as a score-settling campaign between different factions.

While Xi's anti-corruption campaign has reached deep, it has spared several prominent targets. Bo Xilai was one of the most prominent of the "Princeling" party in Chinese politics. The Princelings are the descendants of distinguished members of previous generations of leadership in the Chinese party-state. Though they do not share a coherent factional view, they have some of the same backgrounds, upbringings, and interests. Many of the Princelings who rule now would have seen their parents rule China a generation ago.

For example, Bo Xilai's father was Bo Yibo, who was one of the most potent leadership figures during Deng's reign of power and was a member of one of the "Eight Elders" who, along with Deng Xiaoping, ruled China as it went through the "Opening Up and Reform" period. Xi Jinping's father, Xi Zhongxun, was also seen as an essential member of this leadership generation. While Bo Xilai's shocking scandal meant the downfall of one of the most prominent Princelings, many of the Princelings still have a lot of influence within China's government.

The Chinese party-state is set up to have income flow to the top: income inequality has been very high, mainly as a result of an urban-rural divide. Much of China's economic growth thesis relies on an increasingly urbanized population. There is an enforced geographical system called the *hukou* system, which limits the internal mobility of workers. This provincial registration system does not allow people to flock freely to the wealthiest areas of the People's Republic of China. For example, Shanghai *hukou* registrations are almost worth their weight in gold: people return to China from North America to ensure they maintain their status. Workers who can go to favored urban areas often are willing to submit to poor labor conditions and wages to "ascend" from the bottom. Unions are unions in name only: the party runs them, and they serve as another layer of political training and political control for the rural workers coming in.

It is also a reflection of a party infrastructure that needs to deliver for its members. Chinese income inequality was significantly higher than that seen in the United States and ranks one of the world's highest.[58] The Chinese political structure enforces a regional distribution of wealth, with different regions benefiting differently. When Xi Jinping rose to power, the provinces he touched were expected to benefit, and there has been a regional difference between provinces affected by the anti-corruption campaign and those that are not—for example, Guangdong, long known for having a more liberal stance on political freedoms and with issues of lingual autonomy, has been hit particularly hard by Xi's anti-corruption campaign.

As Xi Jinping has consolidated support around him and his position of "core leader" has become more and more entrenched,[59] wealth for the party has flown more and more to his loyalists. Family members of powerful elites have accumulated large fortunes due to the political prestige of their family members. But when Xi's family was highlighted for this in a Bloomberg report, Bloomberg was banned from the Chinese mainland. Eventually, the economic pain this caused may have led to Bloomberg taking down the report—reporters who were part of the team behind the research talked about getting death threats.[60] Statements taken from the editor-in-chief of Bloomberg showed that he was nervous about reporting on the regime precisely because Bloomberg might be kicked out of the nation.

The anti-corruption efforts received a boost when Xi Jinping announced that he was looking to crack down on "tiger and flies" within the party. While it is murky who is targeting whom and which faction of power may gain from whose downfall, it is undoubtedly clear that the enforcement action in keeping party members reined in and possibly imprisoned is coming from the CCDI.

During Xi's first term under its former head, Wang Qishan, the CCDI went after ex-members of the Politburo Standing Committee, showing that Xi was not averse to going after even the most powerful men in the Chinese party-state below him. The anti-corruption drive has reached deep within the halls of Chinese power. In 2023, senior members of the Chinese party-state, including the foreign minister, the defense minister, and those in charge of China's nuclear arms have disappeared from public view. Li Keqiang and loyalists to Hu Jintao were seemingly sidelined. It has also been applied sector-by-sector, with hospital chiefs, tech entrepreneurs, and anybody seen as creating too much wealth for themselves as possible targets.

While a lot of the focus of the regulatory party-state has been on reining in the financial excesses of the Chinese people and cautioning how Bitcoin is an unwise financial investment, this is another sensitive point where Bitcoin could intersect. Bitcoin plays a role here since a primal focus and weakness of the Chinese Communist Party is the tendency of its elite members to stash their wealth and even sometimes their family abroad in fear of arbitrary and somewhat frequent political reprisals. China's capital controls are designed partially to keep funds within the country, but also to keep people seen as corrupt in check. For example, a slight loosening in 2008 caused investment in foreign real estate and shifts in American real estate prices, as Chinese nationals sought to hedge themselves from the control of the Chinese Communist Party.[61] With Bitcoin, people can opt out of this system and hedge against it somewhat as they move themselves and capital with them into other countries.

Operation Fox Hunt and Operation Sky Net have been the Chinese party-state's response—going outside of its borders to enforce its laws on those who have escaped from the system and are seen to be corrupt. Thousands of Chinese nationals who have moved overseas and have been convicted of financial crimes in the Chinese system have been convinced to come back through shadow-and-dagger means.[62] While the United States and China have no extradition treaty, there are cases where both authorities cooperate with one another, with the United States deporting certain targeted criminals to China. That hasn't stopped the Chinese party-state from sending undercover teams to stalk some overseas Chinese nationals and try to convince them to come back to China to face the Chinese state's version of justice. This has involved everything from harassment to leveraging any family ties in order to persuade people to return.

The nature of anti-corruption has deep implications across Chinese society. The Chinese party-state sees it as a central priority and has imprisoned senior party members for everything from accepting bribes to having affairs in order to make examples of them. The party wants to maintain its one-party rule by portraying itself as a moral and economic exemplar. Its socialist legacy has destroyed the idea of a spiritual afterlife, and so its "mandate to rule" comes from being able to provide material wealth to the Chinese people. Xi Jinping sees corruption as a central threat to the Chinese Communist Party's existence—a party that is bent to his will in a way that has not been seen since the death of Mao. Even though the crackdown has been unprecedented, the perception of economic elites and party cadres drawing massive benefits and living lavish lifestyles is the one threat to Xi's control that he cannot transcend quite yet.

Just like inflation, corruption has led to massive political turmoil in China. Part of the reason for Nationalist China's fall to the Communist Party was the corruption present in the system from elites siphoning wealth. China's economic rise has given many more material benefits—yet those benefits can lead to the Chinese Communist Party's downfall if the inequality present in the system breaks out into protests and dissent. In order to prevent this outcome, the Chinese Communist Party has sought to reach beyond borders and into new technologies like Bitcoin to plug every possible hole it can in its defense. Because of the nature of Bitcoin's peer-to-peer and uncensored approach, it represents the antithesis of the controlled state economy and the yuan. As such, Bitcoin offers a legitimate hedge and a way for Chinese citizens to get their money and finances outside of the hands of the Chinese Communist Party—something that is existentially scary for the Chinese party-state. Bitcoin can act as a "scarecrow" where Chinese concerns can register worldwide. The Chinese party-state tends to use financial crimes to justify its overseas hunt for people who have escaped from the Chinese party-state system. Given Bitcoin's murky reputation, it may have found an angle of attack to focus other nation-states doing its bidding—even deep rivals (after all, CZ from Binance was never arrested by the Chinese authorities but was eventually done in by the American judicial system).

Environment

In its environment and energy policy, the Chinese party-state has also found another angle of attack that can help rally even its deepest nation-state rivals. The environment is why China cited the need to ban Bitcoin mining in the first place. The Chinese party-state likes to paint itself as a conserving force regarding the environment. One of the cornerstone achievements of Xi's administration is the relatively cleaner air present in the 2010s and 2020s versus the chronic smog that plagued most Chinese cities. Xi's China wants to paint itself as a force acting against climate change in a top-down direction. Nevertheless, while air quality has improved and emissions have leveled off somewhat, Chinese carbon emissions are still ongoing, and the Chinese party-state is building large coal projects. In debates about the environment, the Chinese state is hiding its central critique about Bitcoin: whether or not it should be considered valid.

This conflict area has been one that has followed Bitcoin—and even though carbon emissions and the environment at large are global issues, it was really in China, which hosted the majority of Bitcoin mining, that these arguments were first sharpened. Due to the proof-of-work system involved in mining, Bitcoin requires considerable volumes of computing power to secure the network. While computing power tends toward where energy prices are lowest or zero, it is not a perfect transfer. Isolated on the cost side, one can quickly see that Bitcoin is consuming power equivalent to a small nation-state. However, the energy basis of proof-of-work makes sense if you want a decentralized security policy for a cryptocurrency. Since Bitcoin mining is dynamic—i.e., it becomes more challenging to mine the more devices are dedicated to it, this acts as a forcing function for new players to shift in if they can and, by definition, tends to break monopolies more quickly. Proof-of-work allows for mobile power demand that moves to use stranded power and power generated from waste. For example, the wasted energy from flared methane gas can be converted to power Bitcoin miners. While whole towns cannot move to be next to the most efficient power source, a trailer filled with Bitcoin miners can. However, how Bitcoin is architected means it will consume power from the nodes storing the many transactions available to the miners that have to deal with a dynamic, adjusting network.

Other cryptocurrencies claim they can avoid this using a proof-of-stake system, where people holding the underlying tokens can "validate" transfers. There is no mining involved or proof-of-work. However, this system also means the governance structure is fixed. Ethereum, for example, had a pre-mine, meaning the founders gave out tokens to certain key members and influencers before the initial coin offering. Solana started with a private token sale to prominent VCs. This initial stake means that proof-of-stake eventually evolves to whoever had an ownership structure at the beginning profiting off it.

Other altcoins like Ripple might claim they are environmentally friendly, yet the question has to be asked: How many alternative monetary systems does the world truly need? Moreover, what can blockchain do that something like Amazon Web Services cannot for most use cases being forced onto a blockchain today?

An essential element of this discussion is that China has increasingly weaponized Bitcoin's energy expenditure as a reason for crackdowns. Chinese courts have ruled that since Bitcoin takes "wasteful" energy to mine, it should not be used for transacting value and should be invalid.[63] The European Union and some American states also embrace the argument presented here by China. Papers by Chinese scientists have asked for shifting from carbon taxes to outright site bans,[64] something the Chinese party-state has pursued. This faultline between Bitcoin as "wasteful" and nation-state regulation will only grow stronger as time passes.

China is the foremost nation-state model in the world that looks to grow its economy through a techno-nationalist approach. State venture funds and companies guided by it invest money and effort into "chokepoint" technologies in China's attempt to leapfrog rivals such as the United States. The party has always been sensitive to allowing the Chinese economy some free rein while firmly establishing political control over its members and broader Chinese society. Its areas of conflict with Bitcoin, from its capital controls system, the anti-corruption drive, and the environment, have helped shape one of the most fascinating conflicts of the 21st century—and a model for how states might respond to Bitcoin, from a series of escalating bans to attempts to create their own digital currency.

A Timeline of Bans[65]

As early as 2013, when Bitcoin was still in its infancy, it merited its first "official response" in Chinese policy circles. On December 5, 2013, The People's Bank of China and related financial regulators told banks to avoid Bitcoin transactions. This first foray into the regulation of Bitcoin started a common theme: the party-state regards Bitcoin as a financial risk first and is concerned with the possibility of financial risk and data being unrecoverable from transactions by Chinese citizens.[66]

In this ban, Bitcoin is cited directly (along with its Mandarin name 比特币, roughly pronounced as bi-tuh-bi) as having come to the attention of international markets. It is introduced in its simplest form as "something" that came out of the calculation of computers. The first section of the policy pronouncement then roughly names four of the critical properties of Bitcoin: has no centralized issuer, a limited total amount (a reference to the 21MM BTC cap), cross-border usage without restrictions, and offering "anonymity."

The first clause goes on to emphasize that because there is no "issuer" that the People's Republic of China recognizes behind Bitcoin, it is therefore not a "currency" and should be recognized as a "virtual commodity." That Bitcoin should not be used as "currency" in the Chinese legal context was the beginning of a thread that continues to this day of how the Chinese legal system treats Bitcoin—where Chinese Bitcoin holders have a right to own Bitcoin but can't use it as money.

The People's Bank of China official who signed the notice is Zhang Niannian, who likened Bitcoin exchanges to "casinos" on his Weibo—a consistent theme in how the Chinese party-state has regarded Bitcoin as a tool for destabilizing financial speculation.[67] The first focus of the Chinese party-state probably is familiar: other countries worldwide have focused on investor protection as a common theme for why Bitcoin should be regulated. However, the Chinese party-state has undoubtedly been one of the most aggressive in pushing forward on this theme.

This notice directly results in BTCC's (a Bitcoin exchange based in the People's Republic of China, and one we discussed at length in the third chapter) surprising decision to drop yuan deposits for Bitcoin, a hint of the trouble ahead for the Bitcoin ecosystem in China. Bitcoin miners and exchanges were about to scale exponentially along with Bitcoin's rise, many of them in China's borders. However, this early shot across the bow provides a warning about how the Chinese party-state is likely to repress Bitcoin—years before policy responses from other countries. It's the beginning of trying to block Bitcoin from its effects on the Chinese nation-state—a playbook that other countries would soon follow as well.

On April 1, 2014, Caixin, a privately held Chinese media outlet that focuses primarily on investigative journalism and has several beat reporters on the economic lens, reported that the People's Bank of China asked commercial banks and payment companies to shut down any Bitcoin trading accounts within two weeks. This marks a trend where regulatory notices are then followed by action in the tight Chinese party-state control over the banking sector. It was the first time the Chinese party-state took concrete action on Bitcoin, and marked it as an early mover against Bitcoin.[68]

On September 4, 2017, amid a speculative frenzy in ICOs (initial coin offerings) mostly offered in Ethereum, the People's Bank of China took its investigation of cryptocurrency exchanges into a total ban on initial coin offerings. It suspended coin and token listings and funds were returned to depositors. The People's Bank of China led here with the foremost "financial stability" mantle. While this did not affect Bitcoin holders directly—ICOs were made possible by the ERC-20 standard and Turing-complete programming languages inherent in the architecture behind Ethereum, a totally different cryptocurrency—it presaged broader action on exchanges and services related to Bitcoin and a broader crackdown. At the same time, the hash rate dedicated to mining in Bitcoin was ever-growing, which the Chinese party-state was tracking.

Two weeks later, on September 15, 2017, local Bitcoin exchanges within the People's Republic of China borders were asked to shut down "voluntarily." Exchanges like BTCChina urged customers to withdraw their funds as quickly as possible.[69] Other exchanges, such as Huobi, moved overseas to continue operations. Chinese Bitcoin holders suddenly found themselves at the risk of third-party custody exchanges. The critical point is that a Chinese citizen who held their private keys and used a wallet or cold storage solution would have been fine. However, if they "held" their Bitcoin on exchanges, especially centralized exchanges that act a bit like a bank, and that exchange is forced to shut down, their funds are no longer theirs but in the void.

An exchange ban is a reminder not only for those based in autocracies but also worldwide that governments can attack businesses built in a centralized fashion located on their territory. Due to this ban, Chinese citizens within the People's Republic of China must now use decentralized or offshore peer-to-peer exchanges to acquire and trade their Bitcoin. Many also continue to mine Bitcoin, allowing them access to more anonymous versions of acquiring Bitcoin, though trading it for yuan is more difficult.

On January 2, 2018, a private memo by China's leading financial Internet regulator, the Leading Group of Internet Financial Risks Remediation, suggests that China's Bitcoin mining businesses should start preparing for an "orderly exit," putting pressure on local governments that had been encouraging the sector in order to promote economic growth.[70] The Chinese party-state will bide its time between issuing a regulatory notice and acting upon it. Yet it's clear that the Bitcoin mining sector, which was built in China and dedicated most of the hash rate to protecting Bitcoin within mining pools and physical farms built by Chinese entrepreneurs, is under threat. It would be three years until the hammer would be firmly swung—yet this warning gave some Bitcoin miners the motivation to leave China.

Caixin reported on August 22, 2018, about bans on "blockchain" news accounts.[71] The Chinese party-state incorporating Bitcoin into its relative control over the firewalled Internet is probably the easiest thing it can do, by using conventional keyword scanning to ban public discussions, especially from large accounts, of issues the party wants to censor. Caixin itself is a victim of this—while playing within the Chinese system, it has several times published articles that have exposed censorship and corruption, and as a result, has been pulled from the Cyberspace Administration of China's list of media that can be re-published, severely limiting its reach. On around the same day, there were bans on overseas exchanges offering cryptocurrency from the Chinese Internet. About 124 exchanges were identified with foreign IP addresses. The Chinese party-state could not do anything directly to shut down the exchanges, so it exerted control by pushing them outside of "regulated" Chinese virtual space.[72] Chinese people can still buy Bitcoin, but the easiest way to do so (exchanges) is now prevented through an IP-level block from Chinese authorities, and public conversations on Bitcoin are partially stifled. The Chinese party-state, meanwhile, is acknowledging that Bitcoin is more than just a financial solution some might choose, but an online community that needs to be censored—and that it had to go beyond borders in order to wall up access to Bitcoin.

On October 23rd, 2020, right in the middle of the COVID-19 pandemic, the People's Bank of China issued a short but relevant notice that reemphasized the ban on using cryptocurrencies to replace the yuan in circulation.[73] It again reinforced one of the Chinese party-state's red lines regarding Bitcoin: the defense of the yuan and the promotion of its digital currency pilot, showing a new path forward for the Chinese party-state. Not only will there be censorship and repression of Bitcoin, but the Chinese party-state will try to set standards for central bank digital currencies going forward across the world as the governmental alternative.

On May 18th, 2021, the regulators behind the 2013 and 2017 bans on Bitcoin and ICOs had their statements reiterated by industry groups, with the China Internet Finance Association, the China Banking Association, and the China Payment and Clearing Association emphasizing that Bitcoin isn't a real currency, that the financial sector would not get involved with Bitcoin, and that the industry should self-regulate and make customers aware that Bitcoin prices can be "easily manipulated."[74] This isn't new ground, but it confirms that even though Bitcoin prices have changed, the regulatory notices the People's Bank of China and other regulators issued still hold on the financial industry.

Vice-Premier Liu He's Financial Stability and Development Committee, the most senior on financial regulation for the

Chinese system, warned on May 21st, 2021, that Bitcoin is "passing individual risks into the whole society." He, one of China's Vice Premiers and a member of its Politburo, is the most senior member of the Chinese party-state to comment directly on Bitcoin and the party-state's thoughts in such a detailed manner. Bitcoin mining hub Inner Mongolia was among the first to obey this veiled directive by banning Bitcoin mining in their territory. Other provincial hubs like Xinjiang and Sichuan followed shortly thereafter.

Bitcoin mining had always been more in the jurisdiction of the provinces that make up the People's Republic. Provincial authorities from Sichuan, for example, had welcomed Bitcoin miners[75]—partly a legacy of the large number of stranded hydropower dams in the region (a Maoist legacy) and ambitious "poverty eradication/reduction" goals imposed on the provincial authorities by those on the top of the Chinese party-state.[76] Within a few weeks of He's statement, provincial authorities would implement their bans, enforcing the will of the State Council into action. Sichuan would issue an order to shut down Bitcoin mining shortly after that, with Bitcoin mining farms closed for inspection.[77] Xinjiang would also send a similar notice to Bitcoin mining parks to shut down. The Chinese state also seized Bitcoin mining equipment, putting another damper on mining for those operating large Bitcoin mining farms. For a society built on black and white cats, even though it was able to chase mice in the form of GDP and wealth generation for provinces, Bitcoin was turning out to be a "mouse" too far.

After the ban, the "reported" amount of mining hash rate plummeted to zero within the People's Republic of China. While there was some geographic displacement of Bitcoin miners and some exiles who decided to move to more friendly climes, the "reported" narrative of there being a ban, a decrease in mining to zero, and then a "secret" resurgence makes little logistical sense for an operationally heavy, electricity-based business. It is likely tough to track mining hash rate properties from the public data available—part of Bitcoin's architecture that allows anybody to join the network with just an IP address. Analysts should be wary of drawing too many conclusions from public IP addresses especially when it comes to China.

Almost immediately after the Bitcoin mining teardown, on June 7th, 2021, Chinese state authorities would go after KOLs (key opinion leaders or influencers) who spoke about Bitcoin and other cryptocurrencies by banning their accounts.[78] This is the continuation of the earlier media ban, with Chinese authorities cleaning up conversations they don't want happening. Within the Chinese Internet, nobody is able to stifle discussions entirely. The Chinese party-state might ban public KOLs, but there are always private chat groups (for example, the ones that bring people to trade Bitcoin for Tether and Tether for yuan), and there will always be smaller public discussions and KOLs. However, it's clear that the Chinese party-state has employed multiple layers of repression to try to stop Bitcoin—and has been changed by the process. In December 2023, SAFE, the Chinese state agency responsible for capital controls, also asked for law enforcement to act against Chinese citizens buying and selling Tether in order to circumvent foreign exchange laws. The agency mentioned the famous case of Zhao Dong, once the "king" of OTC cryptocurrency trading and now sentenced to jail for seven years for selling USDT (among other offenses).

Throughout all these bans, the critical fact remains that Bitcoin remained as vital as ever. Even though China was the top host of Bitcoin mining before the ban, it took the network just a few months to recover, with miners settling all over the world, from Texas to Central Asia. Mining hash rate doubled from 2022 to 2023 after first crashing due to the ban.[79] The amount of computing power dedicated to Bitcoin is at an all-time high, but now the world's largest mining pool is based in the United States rather than China. This speaks to the difficulty of enforcing bans on Bitcoin. Across the vast physical expanse of land that the Chinese party-state claims for itself, many still defy it, from using VPNs to mining for Bitcoin.

China's actions tend to have a pronounced effect on the price of Bitcoin, but it has not acted to change the protocol in any way. No government can ban every element of Bitcoin, which is part of why Bitcoin exists in the first place. You can't stop two people from entering a physical trade with one another without either exerting immense physical surveillance and force or blocking off not just individual websites but entire Internet protocols. China's solution seems to be embracing the most aggressive implementation of a central bank digital currency with the lowest transaction fee possible and trying to stifle Bitcoin's growth by banning exchanges and mining, but even this idea suffers from issues with merchant adoption domestically.

From Theory to Practice

In China, opera has been a consistent thread for millennia. The practice goes back to the historical "Three Kingdoms" period. Chinese theater has been around even longer than opera: as early as the Shang dynasty (which stretched back to 1766 BC), dances that symbolized hunting and the hunted animals were performed. The rich symbolism of Chinese theater has influenced Chinese and East Asian history throughout the centuries.

The People's Republic of China is a master at deploying theater. There is the practice of embracing "blockchain" as a frontier technology while scorning Bitcoin. Then there is the real act behind China's reaction to Bitcoin, whether through bans or trying to puff up its central bank digital currency: the digital yuan. In deploying these theater acts, the very nature of Chinese policymaking has changed in its embrace of "blockchain" and a "digital yuan" as frontier technologies to pursue and its scorn of Bitcoin. There is a theory and a philosophy behind actions that the Chinese party-state takes—and when it came to Bitcoin, discouraging its use and encouraging the use of "blockchain" quickly set China on a path to be the leading nation-state in trying to ringfence itself against Bitcoin.

Chinese party-state mentions of "blockchain," the underlying data structure behind cryptocurrencies, are overwhelmingly favorable. In October 2019, Xi Jinping gave a speech wherein he said that China had to seize the opportunities presented by blockchain. At the time, 500 companies had already registered to take advantage of this blockchain support.[80] The split between blockchain and cryptocurrency seems clear: one conveys state data control, and the other evades it. Xi Jinping and the Chinese state want to benefit from the digitization and the control blockchains might offer over their populations while scorning an independent financial tool that erodes that control. The Chinese party-state has been the leader in the global narrative where blockchain is seen as "useful," while Bitcoin is portrayed as useless, stupid, and a scam.

The Chinese government has claimed it has the most "blockchain" patents worldwide. The Ministry of Industry and Information Technology (MIIT) claimed that China held 84% of the world's blockchain patents, with "rapid integration" into economic and government affairs.[81] By claiming that it needs decentralization and distributed data stores to ensure the integrity of the system (rather than a resilient cloud computing solution), China is playing the worst of both worlds when it comes to venture capital, governing at times in buzzwords rather than practical technologies. Instead of a bottom-up development triggered by technologists looking to improve on a technological base and learn, there is a top-down push to embrace and use new technologies to use them in policy pronouncements.

In Maoist times, patents were regarded with suspicion at best, along with most forms of private property. In 1979, after Mao's death, Hua Guafeng, Mao's successor, gave the State Science Commission the mandate to decide all patent-related matters. With Deng's economic reforms, the Chinese patent system has become well-established, and often cited with pride by state authorities—especially when it comes to new technological "buzzwords" and the incredible volume of patents filed by the Chinese Patent Office. The Chinese government encourages more patents to be filed, even if those patents are built on open-source code, and add only incremental value.[82] Indeed, it is a known fact that because the Chinese state valorizes patents so much, a bunch of companies flexing IP and filing patents (in a system where patents cost virtually nothing to file) can only help elevate their standing for Chinese state authorities, which may have no better way to distinguish technological advancement while trumpeting patents as a sign of economic strength.

To investigate who is filing these patents and what they contain, the author has analyzed the blockchain patents in the Chinese system.[83] On Google's Patent Database, as of June 2023, there are about 8,000 patents with the words 块链 or "blockchain" in Mandarin—of which 7,000 were filed with the Chinese Patent Office. About 23,000 patents related to Bitcoin have been filed at the Chinese Patent Office. Meanwhile, in English, there are almost 100,000 results with the word blockchain in them and being filed in the Chinese Patent Office—compared to 41,500 or so for Bitcoin.

The grant date varies widely among the English blockchain patents filed at the Chinese Patent Office. It is only in 2018 that we see more than 1,000 patents with the word blockchain in them granted by the Chinese Patent Office—which is around when Xi Jinping stated in the 18th collective study of the Political Bureau of the Central Committee that distributed ledger technology/blockchain has "many uses" in China. 2022 was the peak year for this sample, with about 9,000 patents granted that contained the term blockchain.

The Stimson Center claims that the primary use case of "blockchain" is as a "cyberattack"-resistant distributed store, yet this skips over why people would run this system in the first place versus working with cloud computing providers or in more elegant ways to protect data that does not connote financial value in of itself. The words "authentication," "encryption," and "safety" are among the most common that show up in Chinese blockchain patent titles.[84] "Storage" is the fifth most common word in all patent titles.

In China, technologies often become a trend in themselves. Entrepreneurs seek new "windfall" technologies to raise state-based financing and venture backing to catapult to new levels of wealth. When the state signals support for a particular industry, it can become quickly elevated: entrepreneurs feel like they can innovate in this new space, and funding from state-based venture firms is sure to follow. Local provinces will start competing to become the "new hub" for a particular technology.

The opposite is true of technologies frowned upon by the Chinese state like Bitcoin. Once the writing is on the wall, legal actions will follow to punish those enabling the technology within Chinese borders. Entrepreneurs received the signal that state support, both financial and political, will not come, and by and large, many chose to vacate the field. It is the Chinese party-state's way of enforcing technological standards and creating what it regards as a "healthy society."

In the West, the Chinese party-state is often wrapped in mystery—Xi Jinping is a central focus because he stands out. Yet he doesn't stand alone—there are other members delegated to handle technical issues. In China, the premier is traditionally the head of the administrative central state: they chair the State Council, which, among other things, is responsible for implementing laws derived from the National People's Congress. The State Council is a collection of agencies and an extension of state power that helps implement the laws passed by the National People's Congress. Through its control over Ministries such as the Ministry of Commerce, it regulates domestic and foreign trade by wielding administrative law. The premier is the head of civic society and the regulatory state; for example, the People's Bank of China, the Chinese central bank, is subordinate to the State Council that the premier heads. The current premier is Li Qiang, widely perceived as a Xi loyalist—while the previous premier, Li Keqiang, was seen as a weak but present counter balance, part of the leadership shift that enshrined Xi Jinping as a unique "core leader" unseen since Mao.

As Vice-Premier, Liu He chaired the Financial Stability and Development Committee and was seen as an economic guru to Xi Jinping. He advocated for a crackdown on Bitcoin and Bitcoin mining, pushing provinces like Sichuan that had first embraced Bitcoin miners as a "green energy" enterprise that could help with poverty into banning them from its borders. An incident involving coal mining in Xinjiang caused a decrease in the global hash rate for the Bitcoin network of around 25%—so at the time, China's actions mattered a lot for Bitcoin's security.

A few months later, Liu He chaired a meeting of the Financial Stability and Development Committee of the State Council. The result was a statement roughly translated as "we should crack down on Bitcoin mining and trading activities and prevent individual risks from being passed to the whole society."[85] Bitcoin had risen to Politburo-level attention and commanded national policy. As recently as a few years ago, the Chinese state did not seem to have extreme views on Bitcoin one way or another. Miners were operating throughout, prominently in Sichuan and

Xinjiang.[86] There was no concentrated oversight: though the Chinese party-state studied Bitcoin to a certain degree, it did not seem like there was a firm policy one way or another that allowed for the rise of a central amount of mining hash power in the physical borders of the People's Republic of China. That stance has changed as the people within the system have changed their views on how prominent Bitcoin is. Minor reservations about financial speculation have broken down into deeper ideological and technological analyses of this technology. In line with a more significant concern about the "disorderly use of capital" and financial stability, a transaction and mining ban on Bitcoin has come to users within the Chinese party-state's physical borders. Nor is this stance likely to change. The people in this system may change as the years go on: the system will inherit new blood while maintaining the same old roles. Xi Jinping will be at the helm for the foreseeable future and the consensus gathered around "blockchain" and Bitcoin will not change much.

A significant departure in the last leadership shift is that of Liu He, who retired from the Politburo. However, he remains in the wings, called upon for his knowledge and experience, especially on trade with the United States and other domestic economic policies.[87] As he has retired, he will not be the front man for future statements on Bitcoin— and to the extent that his influence reigns, it is because of Xi Jinping's trust in him.

Banned by the Great Firewall

One of the ways that the Chinese party-state enforces control is through its tight gardening ring around the Chinese

Internet. This isn't an absolute black and white form of control—the Chinese Internet contains coded messages and KOLs that sometimes counter and undermine the Chinese party-state. However, one of the easiest ways for the Chinese party-state to ban something is to restrict access to foreign IP addresses. Bitcoin is a malleable system that uses many different components and distributed nodes to power—so it's difficult to ban that outright. However, sites that offer Bitcoin content and services are often restricted to a certain IP address—an easy addition to the Great Firewall if needed. The selection of sites banned by the Chinese authorities (and those that are not) gives a glimpse of what the Chinese party-state's priorities are.

As of May 2022, the Chinese firewall is currently banning the website Coindesk, one of the top publications on cryptocurrencies. Though not nominally Bitcoin-focused, it carries several articles on Bitcoin and China and opinion pieces. There are hundreds if not thousands of China-related articles, including extensive coverage of the multiple series of bans on cryptocurrency and Bitcoin, from exchange bans to the mining ban. Coinmarketcap is the world's largest aggregator of cryptocurrency prices and exchanges. The ban on Coinmarketcap in China began during the September 2021 wave of cryptocurrency transactions and services bans.[88] It is possible that the live-time tracking of what the Chinese state considers a "disorderly" use of capital proved too much.

Cryptocurrency exchanges have been banned as well. Coinbase is one of the world's largest cryptocurrency exchanges, with 24-hour volume in third behind FTX and Binance (as of May 14, 2022). Although users can buy and transact with Bitcoin on it, Coinbase has dipped into providing many tokens with a less proven history. A publicly traded company in US equity markets, it should be of little surprise that Coinbase and its domains were banned across the Chinese firewall in May of 2022. The same is true for Binance, the world's largest cryptocurrency exchange by trading volume. It has held a dominant position for many years, helping its founder, Chengpeng Zhao (CZ), amass a fortune worth dozens of billions of dollars. Though founded in the People's Republic of China, Binance's headquarters has changed numerous times as crackdowns have followed on Bitcoin and then on cryptocurrencies.

It has not been just Bitcoin and Bitcoin-related domains that have attracted the wrath of the Chinese party-state. Other adjacent technologies have been banned, including encrypted email provider ProtonMail. Bitcoin's ban has some critical differences, making it unique. Andy Yen, CEO and co-founder of Proton, a privacy-based suite of tools that runs from email to VPNs, remembers the time well. With an office in Taipei, he carefully monitors the region's situation. As he puts it, "At Proton, [the Chinese party-state] did not come up and say Proton is banned. The Russians did, right? The Chinese did not do that; they just simply made it hard to access from beyond the firewall."

Interestingly, CasaHODL, a Bitcoin custody and security solution with a mobile wallet, resources, and accessories surrounding Bitcoin security and a multi-sig authentication scheme is not currently banned. Nor has *Bitcoin Magazine* been banned, which is filled with ardent long-form thought pieces about Bitcoin, its history, technology, and philosophy (an English-focused publication that often references more niche topics is likely one that has not gotten noticed yet)—and which is hosting an event in Hong Kong.

Unlike other technologies with centralized servers, Bitcoin access is still not denied in China. Like Proton, there are escape hatches for willing Chinese netizens, though, with Bitcoin, seemingly more and more obstacles pop out daily. By nature, the technologies are different. Bitcoin holds monetary value and is protected as virtual property by Chinese law. It is also more difficult to ban a decentralized protocol; for example, people in China can still buy or sell Bitcoin through Tether or peer-to-peer networks.

Different parts of the Bitcoin ecosystem would have to be part of a ban—it is more complex than letting people not access a specific IP. Bitcoin relies on the same networks of broader communication as the Internet. Banning Bitcoin would involve banning layers of network communication— and since Bitcoin can interoperate between different protocols and is spread over many different IP address agents contributing to mining, buying, and selling Bitcoin, it is more difficult to ban Bitcoin totally. For example, a nation-state can ban all of the multiple IPs that serve Bitcoin content or serve as Bitcoin exchanges, but it would be tough to maintain that. Theoretically, anybody with Internet access and communication methods can buy or sell Bitcoin with others under the right circumstances. Nobody can block the underlying action of sending value over the Bitcoin network, any more than they can censor transactions without attacking the whole system and network.

For example, Proton can be accessed with the right VPN. This private network allows somebody to disguise their

Internet traffic through another location. Using this allows Chinese netizens to access not just Proton but the Internet beyond the Great Firewall. VPNs, however, are illegal in China. New regulations in 2021 go so far as to penalize companies that host app stores for providing VPN apps or anything that allows Chinese citizens to circumvent the Great Firewall.[89] The most famous enforcer of these laws might be the one company that has chosen to go deep in its commitment to do business with the Chinese party-state: Apple.

Apple has been "the only company willing to do a deal with the devil," according to Yen. While other American companies like Facebook/Meta are banned in the Chinese firewall, Apple manufactures many of its iPhones in mainland China. It also maintains its app store, including a Chinese version where thousands of apps disappear according to the whim of the Chinese party-state.[90] The cost of being the world's most lucrative company is the balance required to placate the Chinese state, from obeying its regulations in cyberspace to keeping data on Chinese servers.

The intersection between this and Bitcoin is quite clear. Damus, an app built on Nostr, is an attempt to open communications between different users according to a similar decentralized network of relays to the nodes that power Bitcoin. Because Damus accepts tipping through the Lightning Network, Apple has banned it for violating its policy on third-party payment systems that do not give Apple a marketplace cut of 30%.[91]

William Casarin is the creator of Damus and has first-hand experience with how the Chinese party-state banned his application, similar to how it tried to go after Bitcoin.

He first got a hint of trouble when the Chinese party-state requested to take Damus off the Chinese app store almost immediately after he launched it. He hypothesized that it was because the Chinese party-state had algorithms ready to ban certain apps that might reach a certain threshold of Chinese users at once—though the lurking thought that the Chinese party-state might have agents set up to monitor the Nostr ecosystem and Bitcoin at large remains. Casarin described an instance where Jack Dorsey's security team banned the entrance of somebody suspected to be a Chinese party-state security agent.

After Apple complied with the takedown notice, most Chinese users flocked to the Hong Kong app store, where it was at one point the top social app downloaded. Bitcoin and Nostr are different, so this cat-and-mouse game unfolds differently, even if the intent is still the same. Nostr does not transmit money; it transmits data. Zap Notes in Damus allows people to send each other Lightning payments, but users do not have to activate it to use Damus. Casarin has noticed that all of the Chinese users he knows about do not use the feature—which makes sense because this is the use of Bitcoin that the Chinese party-state most penalizes.

Regarding the data and communications sent to different users, Nostr uses regular web sockets, which makes the traffic from Nostr the same as the signals from "regular" web traffic. It operates like email in this regard, making it much harder to censor Nostr and Damus messages without cutting China off from the rest of the world regarding Internet traffic. It also allows people within the mainland to access Nostr and Damus messages without using a VPN—handy for an environment where VPNs are technically still illegal while offering unsteady and slow traffic at best most times.

However, the Chinese party-state was not finished. Nostr works by broadcasting information across the network through a series of relays. The relays are local servers that can created with different settings, including geo-located ones. Many are based in Japan, where they might restrict access to people with IPs within Japan, allowing somebody to log in and get messages in the language of their choice and closer to local locations—Japanese relays serving Japanese users. This setup also allows for a censorship-proof way to get and transmit messages from the global Nostr network—though it does not come without physical risk of arrest, for example. Damus was the most popular way for Chinese nationals to access the global Nostr communications network. The Chinese party-state banned the bootstrap and default relays that Damus used, showing that it was directly tracking Damus and finding ways to disrupt its usage. Damus has since set up countermeasures, but that shows that even foreign and open-source apps are subject to the mouse-and-cat game with the Chinese party-state that happens within the Great Firewall.

The future of the world's technological development might look like different companies loyal to their geographical sphere and organizations playing cat-and-mouse games with various nation-states. Those rare companies that can transcend tech cold wars between different world powers might be compromised by all rather than by none—as we might have seen with Apple. The addition of Nostr makes this a broader open-source "freedom-tech" discussion, where people will have to choose between either technology controlled by nation-states through companies within it or free technologies built for worldwide use, replication, and more—from speech to money.

When the State Council and Zhang He announced their stance on Bitcoin mining, it pushed some Bitcoin mining entrepreneurs out of the country and toward other locales such as Texas.[92] There is no doubt that there is still some Bitcoin mining happening within China: after all, only hardware devices, Internet access, and a source of power are needed, and where Bitcoin mining occurs can only be primarily traced by IP address, which anybody can manipulate to show whichever geography they want (this is why it appears there is a significant quantity of Bitcoin mining activity in Germany, host to many Tor servers when that is unlikely for physical reasons like power prices).

On June 26, 2023, a Chinese court ruled that a contract for the sale of Bitcoin miners represented an investment in "virtual currencies" and, therefore, was against Chinese law, which again emphasized that the State Council's statement on Bitcoin mining resonates throughout and that from it, actual policy affecting Chinese citizens and Bitcoin will come down.[93] It again made clear that China was not a friendly policy environment for proof-of-work Bitcoin mining.

Conclusion: The Trouble with Bitcoin

Bitcoin's legal status means the Chinese state is not trying to seize Bitcoins that Chinese citizens and residents own. Smaller chat groups and over-the-counter exchanges exist so that people can purchase Tether from yuan and trade that Tether for Bitcoin if they wish. Recently, in Hong Kong, with a judicial system following mainland desires and wishes more and more with each passing year (and with the pro-democracy political opposition largely resigned to the sidelines of power or under arrest), Bitcoin was also declared virtual property—which brings Hong Kong to a similar standard to China's stance on Bitcoin.[94] In May 2022, this stance was reaffirmed by the Shanghai High People's Court, which, despite the history of bans on Bitcoin-related transactions, clearly stated that Bitcoin confers economic value to its holders and that it can be held and disposed of by those holders. Therefore, it was entitled to protection by the authorities.

The party has decided not to actively attack Chinese Bitcoin owners and try to seize their funds. The Chinese party-state is centrally focused on Bitcoin not displacing the yuan—thus, the pilots around the e-CNY and state incentives for its adoption. The closed Chinese system of capital inflows and outflows escalates this priority. Any use of Bitcoin as a currency and a medium of exchange is invalidated by Chinese courts—yet some of this activity still happens under the surface. And so Bitcoin continues to survive in China—but hidden away.

Chapter Five

The Digital Yuan

It is in China where electronic cash standards will likely be defined. Through its new digital currency, China aims to displace domestic tech giants, grant (more) control to the financial sector and the party-state, and internationalize a set of standards for central bank digital currencies.

Digital central bank currency is very different from cryptocurrencies like Bitcoin. Instead of relying on a peer-to-peer network of demand, digital currency takes the state's authority and tries to implement it in a digital format. Bitcoin is not backed or issued by a state. In the standards the People's Bank of China (PBoC) is trying to set for the rest of the world, it is clear that the Chinese party-state has identified Bitcoin as a primal threat—and wants to insulate itself and other countries from it by offering a central bank digital currency standard.[95]

What Is Driving the Digital Yuan

The battle for monetary supremacy today is being fought on the digital plane. The PBoC has counted on the United

States to remain complacent at best—and to scoop up countries that are disaffected from the US-led world order to start and pilot their CBDCs. In 2016 the PBoC launched a Digital Currency Research Institute and had the approval of the State Council in 2017 to develop a digital yuan in conjunction with authorized bank partners.[96] The research institute is composed of veteran regulators and bankers rather than technologists, and as a result the e-CNY offers a different technology and a philosophy other states might follow. The e-CNY changed from taking a blockchain and decentralized ledger approach to one using a more centralized ledger. A country's central bank would issue digital currency like the digital yuan rather than the stateless origin of cryptocurrencies like Bitcoin.

This difference in approach drives significant differences beneath the surface. For example, data privacy and system privacy can be designed with third-party tools in Bitcoin but are unlikely to be enforced appropriately in a state-driven system. The creators of the apps and tools involved with the digital yuan are likely to be centralized and approved by the central bank rather than an open-source ecosystem. While the central bank insists that interest rates will not be part of the e-CNY, it is perhaps fodder for future or other versions of CBDCs.

Most importantly, centralizing allows for tracking, and punishing somebody in light of digital data is nothing new in the People's Republic of China. The Chinese Communist Party has imprisoned more than 50 people for posts on overseas social media that are technically illegal for anybody within the mainland to access. The Chinese authorities arrested Zhou Shaoqing from his home after posting something critical of the Chinese Communist Party and its COVID-19 policy—to 300 followers on a foreign social media network. He was sentenced to nine months in prison. Sun Jiadong received a 13-month term in December for posting on Twitter, to all of 27 followers, "Glory to Hong Kong, shame on Communist bandits."[97] A party-state that can reach down all of the way to citizens posting on a public social media network that is not even based in the country is one that is looking to leverage its access to virtual and financial data to maximize its control.

Nor is this trend confined to mainland China. In Hong Kong, for example, protesters opted for cash payments for single tickets after Hong Kong police described their reusable Octopus cards as mobile GPS. Moreover, among the Chinese diaspora, Zoom cut off rooms hosted by Tiananmen student leaders at the behest of the Chinese government.[98] Different states have their version of the surveillance state—attempts to defeat end-to-end encryption (for example, the NSA's backdoors into critical technology). What makes the Chinese version increasingly threatening is its massive scope and reach, its ascendant formula for international authoritarian technological management, and the Chinese state's proclivity to crisis management that borders on imprisoning anybody tweeting a certain way or who caught COVID-19. The Chinese party-state weaponized the COVID-19 codes that allowed people to travel or not to punish bank protesters in Henan. WeChat and Alipay, technologies that the Chinese state wants to centralize further, are already known for censoring individuals and bringing them to the attention of police and state authorities. For example, WeChat has banned people from sharing articles critical of the Chinese Communist Party even if they are outside of China.[99] It can be easy to see a world where people are banned from the digital yuan or its "airdrops" or coupons based on their behavior—and one in which it becomes one of the only modes of payment left in China.

The digital yuan also differs from digital payments run by private companies in the PRC such as Alipay. The first primary reason is that the digital yuan is not just an interface for bank deposits; it has the standing power of currency in China's borders. Merchants must accept payment in digital yuan. Since the digital yuan is another layer of money issued by the central bank, it also means that Chinese citizens do not need a retail bank account to access it, unlike with WeChat or Alipay. This allows for higher-order trials with JD.com, a major Chinese tech company, experimenting with payroll in digital yuan and banks being able to transcend the limits placed on Alipay and WeChat.[100]

Displacing Private Companies

The digital yuan brings data and control even closer to the state by displacing the private companies that currently own China's payments ecosystem. Chinese state authorities investigated both Alipay and Tencent (Wechat's parent company) for anti-trust violations.[101] While China's digital economy has grown mainly on these two digital payment rails, the government wants both companies to hold less power than they currently do. When Jack Ma famously made statements that pointed out the glaring inefficiencies in China's lending system, Ant Financial (which he had rolled Alipay into) was no longer allowed to go ahead with its IPO, and Ma himself disappeared for several months before reappearing in a strange form of exile.

The Chinese state aims to monitor different financial transactions and register wallet users using the "one coin, two ledgers, and three centers" system, creating an automated KYC/AML system that can extend internationally. It shifts the onus of retail payments onto the retail banking system, which the Chinese system has long used for its goal of capital consolidation in terms of loans. One of the PBoC's explicit goals is to "provide a backup or redundancy for the retail payment system." However, this comes at a cost: the banking system is not necessarily designed to deal with the cybersecurity and scale implications of digital payments. Witness the cyberattack that hit the American unit of the Industrial and Commercial Bank of China (ICBC), China's largest bank, and forced it to trade via USB sticks.[102] In another branch of government, the massive database of personal data the Shanghai police was holding onto of around 1 billion people's data was exposed to the world.[103]

The Chinese state thinks its version of GDPR, the Personal Information Protection Law (PIPL), will protect against data consolidation and hacks like this. However, PIPL follows a trend of keeping data within domestic providers, with companies remotely friendly to China, such as Yahoo and LinkedIn, having to shut down.[104] PIPL is unlikely to restrain the Chinese party-state's usage of data in any meaningful way—and instead serves as a blueprint for overtly retaining data on Chinese servers that can be accessed on every element of a Chinese citizen's life: from their locations (tracked by COVID QR codes) to their financial transactions—in sharp contrast to the way Bitcoin is secured by game theory, open-source technology, and global audits enforced by peer-to-peer value. PIPL also tracks the Chinese party-state's belief in the partners within its ecosystem it can control: prioritizing putting data into private Chinese or ideally semi-public Chinese entities that obey the party, and choosing sectors like the banking sector that have been reliable from the start to maintain the financial and data system the party prefers—especially in the light of a technology sector that has been seen as more and more unreliable.

Table 2 (*opposite page*): Which Chinese banking partners work with the e-CNY

The Digital Yuan Pilots

The digital yuan is a priority for the state planners of the People's Republic of China. In 2021, the PBoC piloted the digital currency to fifteen provinces and twenty-three cities.[105] There has also been growth in commercial banks, creating exchanges where people can buy the digital yuan and encouraging cities and provinces to accept taxes paid in the digital yuan. Though merchants have yet to roll it out full steam, the government is trying to encourage usage. By putting pressure on significant parts of the Chinese digital economy, there is a path to broader adoption beyond paying governmental fees and party dues. And by providing a solution for merchants without any transaction fees to the payment ecosystem, the Chinese party-state is trying to prepare for an era of more automated payments between humans in the future who want to exchange digital value with each other.

Bank	Description
ICBC (Industrial and Commercial Bank of China)	As of December 2022 the third largest bank in the world by market capitalization—deemed a "systematically important bank" by the Financial Stability Board.
Agricultural Bank of China	Part of China's "big five" banks. It hosted the world's biggest IPO at the time in the mid-2010s.
Bank of China	Fourth-largest bank in the world by market capitalization and a member of China's "big five" banks.
China Construction Bank	One of China's "big five banks." Bank of America paid a 9% equity stake in 2015 for $3B but eventually divested entirely.
Bank of Communications	The smallest of China's "big five banks."
Postal Savings Bank of China	Focused on rural and low-income customers.
China Merchants Bank	China Merchants Bank has one branch in Hong Kong and another in New York City.
WeBank	The banking service associated with WeChat Pay.
MyBank	The banking service associated with Alipay.

You can only use the e-CNY app if you're in one of the pilot cities covering many of China's significant "Tier 1" cities. This list of pilot cities includes:

- **Shenzhen** is a metronym for China's technological development and is known as a "tech hub" in China.
- **Suzhou** is a city in Southeastern China close to Shanghai and is a significant hub for manufacturing.
- **Xiong'an**, a development hub for the Beijing area, is expected to be populated by many state-owned enterprises and agencies built under the direct supervision of the State Council and the central government.
- **Chengdu** is the capital of Sichuan Province and the fourth-largest city in China. It is the westernmost gate city for China before bridging out to Tibet and Xinjiang.
- The **Beijing Olympics** site marks China's need to appeal to tourists and foreigners and use marquee events to speed up e-CNY usage.

In November 2020, the PBoC added the following cities to the list.

- **Shanghai**, the commercial capital of China, is China's genuinely global city.
- **Hainan** is often a domestic tourism hotspot due to its beaches and warm climate. Sanya, the southernmost spot in Hainan, is famous as a vacationing hotspot.
- **Changsha** is a historical city and the capital of China's Hunan province, where Mao Zedong was born.
- **Xi'an** is a city in China's center leaning to its west and the ancient imperial capital during dynasties such as the Tang Dynasty. China's first emperor, Qin Shi Huang, is buried here with the famed terracotta warriors.

- **Qingdao**, perhaps most famous for its namesake beer and brewery, is a city on the Eastern coast of China.
- **Dalian** is a city and major port close opposite to the North Korean shore.

In 2022, the People's Bank of China added the following cities on top of the original "core" ten cities that started the e-CNY pilots:

- **Fuzhou**, the capital of Fujian province, is ranked one of the fastest-growing cities in the world by the Brookings Institute. Xi Jinping was the governor of Fujian from 1999 to 2002.
- **Tianjin** is a major port city in northern China, close to Beijing. It is one of the four cities in China, along with Beijing, Shanghai, and Chongqing, that are significant enough to be directly administered by the central government of the Chinese party-state rather than a provincial government.
- **Guangzhou**, part of the "Greater Bay Area" of China, is trying to construct around Guangdong-Hong Kong-Macau, which Chinese state planners want to advance as a leading global region.
- **Chongqing**, a major metropolis in the Southwest of China, is one of the four cities directly administered by the central government. It covers a large geographic area similar to some countries. Before his downfall, Bo Xilai, a rival to Xi Jinping, was the Party Secretary of the metropolis.
- **Xiamen** is a significant city that is part of the Fujian region Xi Jinping used to govern and is right across from Taiwan.

Six cities in the **Zhejiang** province were close to hosting the Asian Games during the pilot expansion. A significant priority of the People's Bank of China has been getting the e-CNY into the hands of foreigners, who are otherwise hard-pressed to interact with the Chinese banking system and digital payments ecosystem. Xi Jinping was governor of Zhejiang from 2002 to 2007. The six cities are Ningbo, Wenzhou, Jinhua, Shaoxing (famous for its cooking wines), Huzhou, and Wenzhou. After the Winter Olympics, the PBoC confirmed that the capital, **Beijing**, and **Zhangjiakou**, the sites of the Winter Olympics, will continue pilots of e-CNY.

The PBoC added five more pilot cities on December 16th, 2022. These are **Jinan** (the capital of Shandong province), **Fangchengguan** (the southernmost port in China), **Kunming** (the capital of Yunnan province), **Nanning** (the China—ASEAN gateway city), and **Xishuangbanna** (bordering both Laos and Myanmar). What unites the last four cities is their proximity to Southeastern Asian countries, from Vietnam to Laos to Myanmar. In total, 29 cities have confirmed a rollout of e-CNY, with one city (Changshu) rolling it out for staff payments of government officials.

So far, digital yuan apps have offered digital lotteries, sponsored by city and provincial authorities, that try to attract people to use the digital yuan. An example of this was featured in Shenzhen's vivacious Luohu district, right across the border from Hong Kong and known for its nightlife and shopping.[106] It is representative of China's proposed growth through Special Economic Zones and top-down planning and a part of the initiative to create a "Greater Bay Area" uniting Hong Kong, Shenzhen, and Guangzhou, the three largest cities in the Pearl River Delta.

The airdrop was called a "红包," a red envelope, the traditional gift given during the Spring Festival. In China, the meaning of getting gifts in a red envelope provides the cultural context to explain an airdrop or the creation of digital tokens. For a week, the Chinese central bank tested the e-CNY application with about 50,000 users getting a digital yuan equivalent of money in the Chinese system. The Shenzhen government prepared the amount for the launch, with 2 million people signing up for the lottery. Each of the 50,000 winners got 200 yuan, or about 30 USD. They could have spent this amount at around 3,400 merchants onboarded for the pilot. Critically, while the digital yuan aims for merchant adoption at scale and by law, an experimental approach to merchant adoption is starting for pilots. Winners were informed by text and were allowed to claim their digital yuan. However, some users reported needing more merchant adoption for their user experience to be optimal. One reported having to drive out of their way to find a merchant willing to accept the digital yuan and needed help finding a restaurant to dine in. Another user bought glasses because they were sold by the only shop nearby accepting digital yuan. Some of this was because the trial was time-capped—there was a week to spend the money.

In many respects, this is similar to the adoption challenges of Bitcoin and Lightning Network. Finding a few spots to spend Bitcoin in major North American cities can be challenging. However, in places like Bitcoin Beach, organic activity from merchants can spur large-scale adoption, and critically, users can use the Lightning Network to interface with merchants through digital payments (like with Bitrefill) and across borders—things you cannot yet do with the digital yuan, and are unlikely to be on the short-term product roadmap. Other trial users discussed whether to use it as an additional app to Alipay and WeChat Pay. Most Chinese citizens will hold the digital yuan to the same user experience that Ant Financial and Tencent delivered—where payments come with minimal friction and any vendor accepts their money.

The Chinese government is aware of this and is taking steps to address these concerns. Foremost is the practical, legal element that says no merchant should deny legal tender, including payments from the digital yuan—a rule not being enforced with overwhelming force now, but the Chinese party-state could quickly move on this front, forcing more businesses to accept it from the ranks of 80 million merchants accepting Alipay. The Chinese party-state is also trying to offer coupons and airdrops to incentivize people to adopt the e-CNY. Meituan, a popular Chinese app for shopping, started offering 20 RMB coupons for the Meituan app to anybody who opened up an e-CNY wallet on the app. A Chinese banking analyst has speculated in Chinese state media that the e-CNY can "boost" consumption and recovery by targeting people with coupons and spending inducements.[107] After all, the People's Bank of China can issue new "physical" cash (known as M0 in technical central bank speak) to anybody they want, and the same is true of digital yuan. Chinese state media is also focused on publishing positive articles about digital yuan, many in English, to impede criticism of the technology.

However, the People's Bank of China has been stymied by international reaction to the e-CNY. It released a whitepaper in 2021 clarifying its position and some of the history behind the digital yuan.[108] It argued that it would not replace physical cash with administrative orders—instead, it sees cash co-existing with the digital RMB. The PBoC's target is clear: the private digital payment rails for the retail class that most Chinese people transact with, the tech companies running those reins, and cryptocurrencies. Mu Changchun, who heads the initiative, has declared at an Atlantic Council event on Digital Currency in China and the Asia Pacific that it should have 100% reserve backing and not merge with the digital wholesale custodian system responsible for the M2 system of broader banking assets.

Challenges Facing the Digital Yuan

Though it is in the pilot stage with no final timeline for a rollout, China's 14th Five-Year Plan highlights the e-CNY. In practice, the technology has rolled out slowly because its core initial target probably finds it difficult to use and not as accessible. The PBoC has identified the unbanked and short-term foreign visitors to China as two manageable segments—but it is unclear that a digital solution like the PBoC's will be a more compelling reason than access to interest rates on their reserves and superior payment networks for the unbanked (the unbanked, after all, have chosen to stay unbanked even with the ability to access Alipay and WeChat Pay). Foreign visitors to China have dramatically declined from about 150 million a year to nearly 30 million a year due to COVID-19 restrictions and gradual decoupling from the global trade system.

From September 2023 onwards, foreigners in China can register for an e-CNY wallet with their overseas phone numbers. Critically, this might mean they do not have as much KYC exposure as Chinese nationals, as not all overseas phones are registered and tied to people's identities.[109]

However, it will be a tradeoff: foreigners in overseas settings will switch to a digital payments ecosystem in return for getting off physical cash that cannot be tracked at all.

Table 3: KYC/data required to access the e-CNY

Tier	Data Required	Access
4 ("Anonymous")	Mobile number (all mobiles tied to personal data in China, though "claimed" Privacy Law protections)	10,000 RMB balance limit, 2,000 RMB transaction limit, 5,000 RMB limit a day 5,000 RMB is ~$700 USD
3	Mobile number and valid Shengfenzen (Resident Identity Card, with registration at local police stations)	20,000 RMB balance limit, 5,000 RMB transaction limit
2	Mobile number, Resident Identity Card, Personal bank account	500,000 RMB balance limit, 50,000 RMB transaction limit, 100,000 RMB limit a day
1 ("No limit")	Mobile number, Resident Identity Card, Personal bank account, Operating agency site	No limits

Alipay and Tencent are used to scaling centralized ledgers to their max. During Single's Days (November 11), a vast shopping and discount spree takes over China. Ironically, created by students who liked that each digit has one (11/11), the occasion has become perhaps the world's biggest shopping spree—almost like combining Black Friday and Cyber Monday. During COVID-19, Alipay had to clear nearly 544,000 transactions per second.[110] In 2022 the e-CNY was aiming to clear just 10,000 transactions per second—and it is not clear that it is used to that capacity most of the time.

On February 14, 2022, at an Atlantic Council event, Mu Changchun claimed that there were a few million RMB a day in e-CNY transactions during the Winter Olympics—a time when the digital yuan was front and center, and the only payments partner allowed to operate outside of Visa (which sponsored the Beijing Winter Olympics). For a point of reference, at its peak, Bitcoin does millions of USD in daily transactions. Alipay can process over 17 trillion dollars of value over a year—netting out to billions of yuan daily in transaction volume. In the same video, he claimed that the People's Bank of China felt the need to start this project in "response to new technologies" (i.e., Bitcoin and possibly Facebook's Libra), and that there were 1.32 million merchants integrated with the e-CNY (as of August 2023, Chinese state media claimed there were 5.6 million merchants). Alipay supports around 80 million merchants as of September 2022, including some overseas from the mainland.[111]

It should not come as a surprise after examining a trial in action that while there have been a ton of activities and free digital yuan handed out, actual usage has been relatively low. For example, two years after launch, a former PBoC research director commented that there were only about $14 billion in transactions.[112] The intent is there, and the People's Republic of China has high digital payment usage, though companies like Alipay and Tencent now carry most of that volume. The process of getting a hardware or software wallet and accessing e-CNY is there, too—and while adoption has been low, it is clear that the intent and the ability to gather data are high. Software wallets are like any standard cryptocurrency wallet—there is a QR code to receive payments and the ability to send a payment. "Dual offline function" seems to require two NFC-enabled devices. Some cards carry e-CNY balances that can pay each other—what the PBoC terms hardware wallets. The PBoC claims to have built most offline technology in-house, but they collaborate with private industry for cellphone equipment and machine learning algorithms.

Table 4 (*opposite page*): What are some apps that currently integrate the e-CNY

The Yuan's Internationalization

The digital yuan will also help with another party-state goal, a more gradual internationalization of the yuan. The Chinese party-state probably believes that a digital dollar and Euro are far behind. By being the first major economy to embrace digital cash standards, China seeks to be the premier currency to have a central bank digital currency and to define what to do with the consolidated financial and payments data. This has been a public goal of the

App	Description
Alipay	Alipay is one of the two sizeable digital payment networks in mainland China, and it has an e-CNY capability.
WeChat	WeChat Pay is one of the two sizeable digital payment networks in mainland China, and it has an e-CNY capability.
JD.com	China's largest e-commerce platform and its equivalent to Amazon, was the first online platform to support e-CNY.
Meituan	Meituan specializes in group-buying and food delivery and had about $30B in revenue in 2021.
Ctrip	Ctrip is a travel platform aggregating deals on flights, hotels, and other travel expenses.
7Fresh	A fresh food grocery chain that planned to open 1,000+ stores in China in the next five years, owned by JD.com.

Chinese party-state since at least 2009, in the aftermath of the Great Financial Recession.[113]

At a glance, the US dollar seems unbeatable. As of the middle of 2021, the IMF noted, however, that the amount of USD reserves held by central banks worldwide had fallen to a 25-year low. Since the EU launched the Euro in 1999, USD reserves have declined from 71% of global central bank reserves to 59%. By factoring out exchange rate fluctuations, central bankers worldwide are still meaningfully decreasing their reserves in USD. The relative trendline will not be sudden and dramatic; it will likely take decades for this to change meaningfully.[114] However, this movement matches the explicit statement of certain central bankers worldwide to get away from USD dominance, most notably Russia's central bank and monetary/fiscal authorities, who are, for example, removing dollar assets from its National Wealth Fund. The Federal Reserve's ability to tame inflation matters a lot here, too. If the American central bank is no longer seen as credible in fighting inflation and its financial decisions are seen to be in tandem with its geopolitical objectives writ large, then there are potent forces for why this trend might continue.

The relative decline of the dollar internationally has also come with a small but noticeable trend in the relative growth of the yuan. A large part of a currency's international attractiveness comes about because of the trade a country conducts across borders. In 2000, the Chinese share of exports was about 4% of world exports, while the United States exported about 12%. By 2001, however, the Chinese state would ascend to the World Trade Organization's trade regime, get access to preferred-country treatment from others, and relax specific tariffs, allowing it to pursue an export-driven path to economic development. In the last twenty years, China has become the world's largest exporter, almost double the share of world trade as the United States has (14.7% for China vs. 8.1% for the United States).[115]

The US dollar punches way above its weight compared to the current share of world trade the United States represents. Part of this is due to the financialization of many products. For example, commodities trading and especially oil trade are often settled in USD even if the two counterparties are not in the United States themselves or settled in the sophisticated markets located (and taxed) in the United States. The yuan still needs to catch up to the US dollar, the Euro, and even the Japanese yen regarding international trade settlements and the foreign exchange reserves of other central banks. The United States draws much of its superpower status from this control of world trade and financial flows. The conflict with Russia shows it is willing to leverage some of that soft power into hard power meant to punish conduct. Cross-border settlements using the SWIFT system usually involve either US-based financial institutions or the approval of either the United States or its allies: cutting out Russian banks from SWIFT shows that the United States, when push comes to shove, will leverage that power against any country it wants to.

Internationalization for the yuan can be seen in terms of offense and defense. The Chinese party-state wants to establish more trade in the yuan in critical commodities needed to feed China's economy: this will also help it deepen political ties with key states. Xi Jinping, for example, has been very vocal about China's willingness to pay for oil in yuan.[116] Whether the Gulf states that underpin the petrodollar would agree is another question—this would be a defining moment in world economics.

The yuan being internationalized has this offensive element: take critical trade goods where the dollar is traditionally the only accepted way to settle and open up the possibility of having the yuan substitute. The Chinese party-state has also tried to use the yuan and dollar substitution to ply potential geopolitical allies away from the American order. Argentina, for example, has been concerned about the runaway inflation of its domestic currency and its dwindling US dollar reserves. Argentina has agreed to pay for Chinese imports in yuan and has activated a currency swap. Many countries are in the situation of having higher debt as well as concerns about their foreign dollar reserves.[117] China's ability to provide goods regardless of what happens to the US dollar and US monetary policy is an attractive proposition that helps keep potential geopolitical allies in the fold.

The digital yuan is an integral part of this. The MBridge connects e-CNY to other central banks.[118] Proposed examples include paying for gas and oil imports with e-CNY—disrupting the role of the petrodollar. In theory, MBridge could also be an alternative system to the SWIFT inter-bank system—which the United States has weaponized against Russia, something that will not be missed in Chinese policy circles. By displacing the corresponding bank system, there is an attempt to bridge financial flows past the American system. The founding members of MBridge include the PBoC, the Hong Kong Monetary Authority, the Bank of Thailand, and the Central Bank of the United Arab Emirates—all coordinated through the Bank of International Settlements. The PBoC has also released a whitepaper on their desire to flow the digital yuan through cross-border payments.[119]

China is also considering playing defense with the yuan. While its treasury holdings are lower now than historical levels, it mostly switched to US dollar debt in different holdings. China is still willing to invest in the US dollar and US-based debt.[120] However, the country is also paying attention to what is happening with Russia, aiming to replicate parts of the Russian strategy to insulate its economy from punishing US-led sanctions, mindful of what might happen with a geopolitical-shattering invasion of Taiwan.

Conclusion: Looking Ahead

China has been changed by its interaction with Bitcoin. Its rich tapestry of "5000 years of history," replete with inflation, empire, kingdoms, and blood, has seen a unique challenge in the bits and bytes that Bitcoin moves. The Chinese party-state has had to create new regulations and rules to try to attack the effect of Bitcoin while having to acknowledge that Bitcoin is worth some amount of value, and so Bitcoin held by Chinese residents should be respected. Its most significant response, though, has been trying to advance "blockchain" as a frontier technology while creating a central bank digital currency, the e-CNY, and a set of standards for other countries to follow.

As Bitcoin emerges to make dissent and civil society more resilient, authoritarian states like China seek to make themselves resilient to encryption and the individual autonomy contained within by digitizing their financial and physical control systems. Which vision will win out depends on their people—whether they embrace this control or seek to hedge against it. In the case of China, which is a controlled society that has undergone two significant protests (in the mainland against COVID restrictions, and pro-democracy protests in Hong Kong), this particular battle is particularly resonant. Perhaps there is no better way to summarize the Chinese party-state approach than Mu Changchun's proclamation in the *Journal of Economic Literature*: "There is no true freedom without discipline."[121]

Chapter Six

Two Protests, One Country

Though protests were rare during China's techwno-nationalist rise, under Xi's rule, two significant policy-changing protest movements occurred just a few years apart from one another—one in Hong Kong for the right to true universal suffrage and the other in mainland China against COVID restrictions. The protests offered the world the first glimpse at how the techno-authoritarian state would handle dissent (including among overseas exiles), the stakes involved—and what role Bitcoin and Nostr can play.

Even though protests and dissent remain rare in mainland China, and the passions of Hong Kong's protests seem to be repressed under new security laws, the opportunities afforded to Chinese nationals to memorize or store a bunch of private keys and have the ability to speak or transact freely is not something that has passed without notice—and there are glimpses of freer communication because of both Bitcoin and Nostr.

Hong Kong

In 2012, schoolchildren took on the government of Hong Kong and the central Communist Party—and won. The Hong Kong government was trying to implement "Moral and National Education"—a version of the post-Tiananmen education that had served the Chinese party-state so well in shaping the views of a generation. The backlash then bloomed into the most severe threat to Chinese state power since the Tiananmen Square Massacre.

The Umbrella Movement came about because of a promise the Chinese authorities had made to secure the handover of Hong Kong. The Basic Law, which serves as the governing law of Hong Kong and its constitution, commits to electing the leader (known as the Chief Executive) by popular vote. No deadline was specified, but some viewed it as a promise that universal suffrage would become the norm in Hong Kong.[122]

While elections were held in Hong Kong for the chief executive role, they were not fully democratic. The Chinese party-state still wielded the power through "functional constituencies" to tilt the balance of votes in its favor. The Chinese Communist Party wanted the power to pre-screen candidates, which many Hong Kongers saw as a violation of their right to hold fair, democratic elections for their leadership. Millions of people marched, protesting what they saw as a rigged 2017 election for Chief Executive.

As the protests continued with the goal of universal suffrage, there were conflicts between protesters and police. Then the local district councils saw a round of voting go toward the "pro-democracy" camp. With elections coming up for the Legislative Council that effectively governs as the legislative wing of Hong Kong, the Chinese party-state had seen enough and imposed the National Security Law, which then led to the arrests of media figures such as Jimmy Lai of Apple Daily and pro-democratic legislators and activists like Joshua Wang. The administration's reaction to pro-democracy protests dented the city's reputation. To this day the Hong Kong administration bans political parties and continues to try dissidents, as the effects of the imposition of the National Security Law asserts its hold on Hong Kong society.

The protesters were not broadly aware of Bitcoin, though there have been instances where the two worlds collided. Some Bitcoin hubs funded supplies and water for protesters, even if it was with Bitcoin Cash.[123] However, while Hong Kongers who protested the administration sought to divest from the Hong Kong dollar and Chinese-tied banking institutions, there was no significant movement toward Bitcoin. Bitcoin ATM usage decreased as protesters filled the streets, and physical Bitcoin users could not access ATMs anymore. It was hard to parse if there was more demand for Bitcoin on decentralized and Hong Kong-based exchanges, but it seemed like there was no particular pattern.

However, once Hong Kong began targeting dissidents for arrest, seizing bank accounts, and placing bounties on specific pro-democracy figures, it has become clear that Hong Kong's control of its fiscal and monetary systems had been weaponized against political dissent—similar to what was happening on the mainland. While it looks like Hong Kong is trying to portray itself as a cutting-edge international financial hub by creating a regulatory environment for cryptocurrencies and regulated "cryptocurrency exchanges," the "One Country, Two Systems" framework that offers some veneer of safety from mainland authorities might have a short expiry date.

Bitcoin's rocky and mixed history with Chinese authorities is part of why Hong Kong has been used as a financial bridge to Bitcoin for many mainlanders, wary of direct conflict with the Chinese party-state. It was this fragile democratic difference between a one-party state and some elections that the United Kingdom wanted to ensure in handing over Hong Kong to the Chinese administration. "One Country, Two Systems" was the compromise, which was meant to ensure that Hong Kong could still have freedom of expression and elections—at a price that led to both the Umbrella Movement and other pro-democracy movements.

It also meant that Hong Kong's law was applied differently from mainland law. Article 1 of the Basic Law makes it explicit that a separate legal system governs Hong Kong until at least 2047, which means that Hong Kong has a separate executive, legislative, and judicial wing (referring to the mainland as the home of the "Central" authorities). As a result, while there is some deference to the central government for many matters, including Bitcoin, banking, and economic restrictions, Hong Kong can still chart a relatively autonomous path.

The Securities and Futures Commission (SFC) is structured similarly to the Securities and Exchange Commission (SEC) in the United States. Virtual assets and tokens are deemed likely to be securities and thus subject to regulation from the SFC, which means that Hong Kong has a unique relationship with Bitcoin: multiple exchanges are either based in Hong Kong or operate there, and mining pools and mining hardware providers still allow Hong Kong IP addresses and Hong Kong mailing addresses to accept their respective wares.[124] Bitcoin is still a part of the city's tapestry, even if official authorities discourage its "unregulated" use.

The Bitcoin Association of Hong Kong hosts meetups and publishes reports on the current status of Bitcoin in Hong Kong (which include a long history of Hong Kong's Bitcoin regulations[125] and a map of places to spend Bitcoin in Hong Kong).[126] There are trading spaces where people onboard customers onto Bitcoin and teach them how to store their wealth. For example, places like Genesis Block served as a portal for bringing real-world wealth into virtual space by offering the ritual of private banking and onboarding to buy tokens and access either stablecoins or Bitcoin.[127] Clients entered the Genesis Block hub and were offered tea and a laptop to begin getting digital assets. This ritual must have been similar to how HSBC might treat a potential client, though it took place in a hackerspace-like setup with plenty of gadgets and Bitcoin-related stickers.

Genesis Block ended up shutting down along with the winding down of FTX, with its founder citing "counterparty risk" as a significant reason.[128] The space promoted FTT, the native token associated with the FTX exchange, and provided guides for purchasing it. FTX once had its HQ in Hong Kong and only moved to the Bahamas in 2021.[129] Some argued that the cash-for-crypto shops like Genesis Block in Hong Kong helped spur the development of FTX, which is why it was headquartered in Hong Kong.[130] However, with the failure of FTX, the impact has been felt worldwide. Hong Kong has lost some of its luster as the Manhattan of Asia, where high finance, expat communities, and financial innovation meet. As the industry decries what happened, Hong Kong's financial authorities are trying to rebuild amid a murky future. They are encouraging Bitcoin conferences such as *Bitcoin Magazine's* Bitcoin Asia conference, offering a cryptocurrency exchange licensing regime, and positioning themselves to offer ETFs with more options than even the American spot ETFs (for example, the ability to withdraw in-kind in Bitcoin[131])—but also regulating physical shops that trade Bitcoin and other cryptocurrencies for cash—a common way to buy non-KYC sats.[132] In this way, Hong Kong (and perhaps the lurking mainland authorities) may be taking advantage of the incredible amount of financial inflows that are coming to Bitcoin spot ETFs as a way to draw foreign direct investment back into Hong Kong—while trying to protect itself from "unauthorized" uses of Bitcoin that could threaten the fragile political balance.

Many Hong Kong legislators now claim that "One Country, Two Systems" is dead. The pro-democracy side has essentially closed shop, their primaries declared illegal, and their legislators in exile, resigned, or in prison. Bitcoin has subsequently and gradually gone from "virtual commodity" to "virtual currency" with more regulatory implications— and you can be sure that Hong Kong's authorities, no matter what their denials, will hew more closely to the sort of policy being implemented on the mainland. In freezing the bank accounts of prominent pro-democracy legislators in exile, civil society groups, and media outlets, and in taking down content critical of Tiananmen Square and in support of the pan-Democratic protests and Umbrella Movement, mainland Chinese authorities are creating a solid case for Bitcoin. While Hong Kong's authorities want to open up a new route for Bitcoin acceptance and regulated exchanges in Asia, there is unlikely to be a core change in China's attitude toward Bitcoin.

Bitcoin's role in dissent has been overrated in the short term but underrated in the long term. In Hong Kong, Bitcoin played at best a marginal role. Some people used Bitcoin Cash to funnel water and supplies to the protesters. There may have been some exchange volume increases on the margin. However, the Chinese party-state's repression showed the need for something like Bitcoin. Hong Kong authorities shut bank accounts and froze funds for pro-democracy legislators and activists. People fleeing the "warlike" state in Hong Kong would have been served well with a rapid way to port their savings across borders.

Mainland China

In mainland China, protests had been rare during the Xi era. While the diaspora reacted to his increasing repression, Taiwanese elected governments pledged to distance themselves from the mainland, and protests sparked thousands to walk through the streets of Hong Kong; within mainland China itself, heavy repression and state support had made it so that any protest was infrequent or nearly empty. During the Arab Spring, there were rumors of a "Jasmine Spring." However, when the American ambassador Jon Huntsman walked around a protest site in Beijing, it was mostly empty. There was not a sustained protest movement.

Dr. Li Wenliang was like many netizens on the Chinese Internet, though he was perhaps more curious about the West than others. In 2019, he registered a Twitter account outside the Great Firewall, though he did not post much.[133] The first account he followed was that of a liberally minded pundit in Chinese politics, Luo Yonghao, who had founded Bullog.cn. Before its bans, the platform was widely known for being a host of liberal bloggers, including Ai Weiwei. Eventually, the platform took on positions that the party could no longer accept, and in 2009 it was shut down in mainland China for good. The only version that survives is now hosted overseas. Li Wenliang was much more of a lurker than a poster—somebody who followed accounts but did not have much to say, which was more typical of the person who "flipped the wall" and escaped the Chinese Internet through a VPN.

People who "flipped over the Great Firewall" tended to fall into three distinct camps: one group was made up of ardent Nationalists, some genuine, and some associated with being *wumao*, or paid 50 cents in order to help advance the Chinese party-state's message in foreign territory. The second group were liberal bloggers and thinkers, many hiding behind anime cartoon profile pictures or something else that kept them anonymous (even on the "Western" Internet, the Chinese party-state has many eyes and ears). The third tended to be those who were curious and who spent a lot more time lurking than anything else. There are variations of this theme; for example, one user on Clubhouse went from being extra curious about people's daily lives to hurling insults over Taiwan and Xinjiang. In general, though, most people will fall under these three groups.

The silent lurkers can sometimes be the most interesting "flippers." Early on, Li Wenliang followed Joshua Wong, who led the student protest movement in Hong Kong. He followed various accounts that showed a liberal streak in Chinese politics that could be dangerous in the mainland. As he built his career toward being a doctor, this independent streak faded from public view. He supported the Hong Kong police and wanted to publicly defend the Chinese party-state's flag in light of the protests. It's hard to tell how he might have thought in private, but at least on the Chinese Internet, it seemed that Li Wenliang was copying the position of the average netizen who felt free to express themselves. In many ways, Li Wenliang was the representative poster of a cat-and-mouse game with Chinese Internet censors, a well-practiced art for millions of Chinese netizens. He might have thought differently, or had different leanings that we would see later—but for a period of time, especially as his career developed, he would post items that would have seen favorable treatment by the Chinese government and many of his peers.

The original SARS epidemic had been a test for the Chinese party-state, whose instinct toward preservation of its power led it to underplay several cases in Beijing. It took one whistleblower doctor, Dr. Jiang Yanyong, to prevent a hidden epidemic from progressing into a pandemic. SARS-1 had a case-fatality rate of around 10-15%, though it did not spread as quickly as COVID-19 would end up doing. However, it left a haunting legacy in East Asia with visions of entire apartment blocks in Taipei and Hong Kong marked for sickness (and often death), and is the reason many people wore masks even pre-pandemic. Initially, Dr.

Jiang Yanyong's whistleblower testimony was a massive win for the nation. He was a role model for speaking truth to power and preventing the Chinese people from unnecessary suffering. The mayor of Beijing and the Minister of Health both resigned because of their actions in hiding the SARS-1 epidemic. The party praised him as a loyal member who had disregarded his safety to advance the nation's interests.

However, he then took his zeal for truth and implemented it in his experience at the 301 Military Hospital as the chief surgeon during the Tiananmen Square Massacre. He asked China's senior leaders to ask for forgiveness from the Chinese people for their actions during Tiananmen and to reassess the event as a patriotic movement. It was a bridge too far for the party, which dared not even discuss the event. Dr. Jiang Yanyong was soon cast out as a disgrace to the nation. Shortly after the COVID-19 pandemic broke out, he would die under house arrest. Dr. Jiang Yanyong's mixed legacy must have weighed heavily on the whistleblower doctors, who were stuck between the truth and making the party uncomfortable. Finally, they released the truth, believing the moment's urgency to be more important than their safety. Dr. Li Wenliang would then be fined for this by the Wuhan police, but his death would ultimately come from working hard to help save others from the virus he had identified.

Online dissent has always been a tricky affair in mainland China. Those with dissident views often play cat-and-mouse with state authorities, hiding behind a veil of netspeak and alternative words. The pandemic sharpened these lines as the Chinese party-state saw little reason to regain its physical control of people while the need for protest and dissent grew stronger. In China, the unique blend of data, machine learning, and tracking was used to enforce the Chinese party-state's survival in front of this new threat. The adjacent technologies to blockchain and digital surveillance were leveraged to their total capacity. Independent media sources who tried to investigate what happened in Wuhan were arrested. Zhang Zhen, an independent citizen researcher, was tortured in state captivity. Online conversations on the topic were strictly locked down. The only place to have been able to have discussions on the topic now would be somewhere like Nostr—where (for example) a post was made by a NPub quoting Zhang Zhen to not let China retreat to becoming like North Korea (and that silence and complicity would be part of that road).[134]

Because of the need to track COVID-19 cases almost religiously, the Chinese state put a QR code system on every phone in the country. This digital tracking system and a daily testing regime allowed the state to track how COVID-19 cases were transmitted. It also offered the most direct way for a police force to track the location of anybody they desired. In the West, police forces can find access to people's location data. However, the combination of the Chinese party-state's forceful COVID testing regime, where living life regularly required updating health status, and the pointed use of technology to control and surveil the Chinese people was unprecedented. Drones, QR codes, and data systems check people's location data and their interactions with one another. Location data and public cameras ensured that dissent could find nowhere to hide. The world saw a glimpse of a digital surveillance state that had nearly no bounds placed on it.

The pandemic allowed the government to leverage data without significant questioning, offering a rare opportunity where the Chinese party-state could deviate from its promise of material wealth. For the last few decades, the Chinese party-state has based its mandate on its ability to deliver material results to the Chinese people. Since the era of Deng and Zhao Ziyang and the death of Mao, socialist ideals have given way to the idea that the party-state's record could be judged by the amount of GDP growth it could deliver. With Xi's ascent and his consolidation of power, the Chinese party-state sought to bring socialism back into the discussion and to stop centrally measuring the party's progress solely by the amount of exports and foreign direct investment that would come in. Anti-corruption would rein in moneyed elites who had grown rich. "Housing," not speculation, would become a tagline targeting the asset where most of the rising Chinese middle class stored their wealth.

COVID-19 soon became the primal focus of the Chinese state. It was cited in state media a record number of times, taking precedence over anti-corruption or the fight between the United States and China that was developing. The Chinese party-state poured money into being self-reliant and developing a native vaccine, a similar dynamic to what is happening with semiconductors now. The Chinese people were also subject to restraints as public travel outside apartment complexes was difficult. Food was a contradictory notion. The ultra-connected nature of Shanghai's tech ecosystem always offered food or anything on demand with a few clicks. Now that same system allowed some to order as much cake as they wanted but not any vegetables or produce. For many of the citizens living in Shanghai in larger apartment complexes, self-organizing communes popped up and used a new form of digital organizing to get food supplies that supplemented the offerings from the government. However, expats and those living in smaller buildings were often left to fend for themselves.

The pandemic also set the stage for China's economy to stumble. China's real estate market came under increasing strain as property developers like Evergrande default on their debt. This slowdown has hit youth unemployment hard—and coupled with demographic restrictions like the "one-child" rule meant that the Chinese party-state has created the conditions for restive protest groups on the mainland and outside of it.

This tension set the stage for a round of protests in Shanghai about the COVID restrictions—one that led to the rapid reversal of draconian COVID restrictions and the digital pursuit and capture of almost everybody brave enough to stand up to the Chinese party-state. China would round up peaceful protesters quietly using new technologies like facial recognition where possible. Its continued consolidation of political power under Xi (and China's recent economic stumbles) has led to discussions on Nostr in Mandarin where Bitcoin is presented as an alternative and hedge. It vividly demonstrated how the Chinese party-state would leverage its techno-nationalist stack from within China—and outside of it on the Chinese diaspora—yet also showed that there were cracks of freedom within that system of control through Bitcoin, Nostr and adjacent freedom-tech if one looked hard enough.[135]

Chinese Exiles

The diaspora has been interested in Bitcoin for many reasons. Some of them see it as a vehicle for dissent and the ability to be freer of the intrusive Chinese party-state, which has gone beyond borders to try to censor discussions about Chinese governance. One of the things that separated Hong Kong from the mainland was the ability to commemorate the Tiananmen Square Massacre. There used to be massive public rallies on June 4th in Hong Kong, with hundreds of thousands coming to Victoria Square Park to light candles and remember. Now that the National Security Law has come into force, these peaceful protests have been quieted and dimmed. But spaces for protest within the Chinese party-state's physical territory are not the only ones under threat. The Department of Justice indicted senior figures at Zoom for disrupting virtual commemorations by Tiananmen Square leaders. Among those leaders was Zhou Fengsuo.

Zhou Fengsuo and Wang Dan (#5 and #1 on China's most wanted list of Tiananmen Square organizers) have both shown that they are sensitive to cryptocurrency and Bitcoin. Wang Dan raised funds using Bitcoin and other cryptocurrencies for the opening of a Tiananmen museum through Coinbase. On his Clubhouse profile, Zhou Fengsuo indicated his interest in decentralization and cryptocurrency. Elsewhere dissidents are researching and translating English-language articles on Bitcoin into Mandarin. On a panel on central bank digital currencies and the digital yuan, Nicholas Yu of the Citizen Power Initiative delved into the workings and operational details of the digital yuan, from what the app looks like and feels like to the surveillance capabilities that the app could unleash on the Chinese people. Badiucao, a dissident artist, has raised money using NFTs of his work. It's clear that even if dissidents aren't super familiar with all of the technology, this larger discussion of Bitcoin's tenets and the offer of the digital yuan has reached dissidents within China and outside of it.

Some people straddle both sides. For example, Chandler Guo started mining for Bitcoin in 2014. However, he now believes many people will use the digital yuan instead because overseas Chinese would adopt the digital yuan—and he believes in the profit motive behind that.[136] Miners, after all, can only believe in Bitcoin insofar as Bitcoin brings them profit. Some of them might believe in the broader tenets of Bitcoin—but they do not have to. Much Chinese discussion about Bitcoin is hidden in technical analysis and price levels.

In the aftermath of these two protests, a stark divide between technology used to liberate and technology used to control has come to the fore as the Chinese party-state imprisons protesters across Hong Kong and the mainland. One can imagine a system where China's state power will determine whether or not citizens can access their funds and grow them—with their ideological purity at stake as well.

Bitcoin has inherent anti-censorship principles: nobody should be denied payments or the ability to make payments in Bitcoin. It is culturally attuned to eroding centralized power, yet large whales hold most of the Bitcoin ever mined. It is, in places, as unequal as the previous system. Its culture is rough and untamed, a vestige of the early

Internet. Adjacent technologies like Nostr extend that philosophy to non-financial spaces and into communication. People can communicate with one another virtually without being tied down to a physical ID that can be used to arrest those expressing themselves—they can find a way outside of the system of technological control and repression the Chinese party-state has built.

Conclusion: Political Repression and Cracks of Hope

In Hong Kong, universal suffrage was a democratic "show," a physical representation of the "blockchain" concept. China offered a mirage of what it meant to have a true democracy. When pro-democracy legislators won, including students from the Scholarism movement headed by Joshua Wong, China chose to undo the election results and impose new standards. The central government sought to write a vision for where democracy could go, with careful guardrails so that it did not stray very far from the party's wishes. When that vision failed, they flipped the table and asserted their true will. Undoubtedly, the same will happen for monetary, technological, and economic systems in a system of one country and two blockchains—and one that is quickly developing the techno-nationalist stack it thinks will allow it to dominate the future. Yet Bitcoin and Nostr offer the ability for Chinese nationals holding a set of private numerals anywhere they want to hedge their bets and to have open discussions about topics where they would be censored on the mainland and possibly arrested. A window of freedom exists here, however narrow.

Chapter Seven

The Techno-Nationalist Stack

The story of Bitcoin and China was never about one technology and one country. To get the whole picture, one must look at the broader picture of the frontier technologies in which China invests. They are part of a philosophical system to enforce China's control over an extreme version of surveillance state capitalism. Few things are more relevant to the themes of this book than China's investment in big data as it seeks to track as much as it can about its citizenry as well as its broader push for technological domination. There is no use generating rich amounts of data if the ability to make valuable insights from it is not present. Data systems would interplay with digital currencies, augmenting their capabilities and, in turn, extracting valuable patterns and individual granularity on different data points. Financial habits are a critical component of a country's data system—these days, "you are what you spend," and a digital yuan system that can help the Chinese party-state track who their citizens are and modify their behavior might be at hand.

Individual-level data from the digital yuan can directly feed data to the party-state, which gives the central bank more authority to track individual spending habits and allows it to retain more control over its fiat currency—but it also might allow for individual-level rewards or punishments, a dangerous idea in a world where disobeying the party carries profound consequences. With machine learning, blockchain, and the social credit system complementing each other, the Chinese techno-nationalist party-state can create ledgers out of the scattered data points in physical space and virtual space, acting with precision and power against individual citizens it deems to be in the wrong while other countries watch or eagerly adapt to what China is doing.

Emergence of the Techno-Nationalist Stack

China's technological rise is based on an engineering-set view of the world. From 1949 to 1985, Chinese university graduates were principally engineering graduates—35% of graduates held engineering degrees versus the 1% who held politics and law degrees.[137] Compare this to the United States, where over half of Senators and one-third of the House have law degrees.[138] China's techno-nationalist rise is no accident.

As a result of increasing college enrollments during the 1970s and 1980s, especially in technical and engineering fields, the leadership class of the Chinese Communist Party is full of engineers.[139] The story of China's technocratic rise reflects this, with Xi Jinping serving as the perfect example. The Cultural Revolution disrupted his secondary education, sending him to the countryside. Eventually, he studied chemical engineering when the Chinese state expected students of all kinds to devote a significant amount of time to class ideology. He fits in the mold of a "technocrat," having had to fit back into the party thanks to his engineering background and persistence in leadership.[140] Xi Jinping trumpets two things as part of his brand: his love for "reading" literature and his heading of "study groups" regarding new technologies of interest like "blockchain" and AI to the Chinese state.

A quick scan of the innovation ecosystem in China shows that the country's leadership, in the name of "common prosperity," is trying to move away from the widespread proliferation of apps, social media, and payment technologies by reining in tech IPOs such as Didi, China's version of Uber. There is now more of a focus on the hardware required to unlock electric vehicles and produce the next generation of semiconductors, as well as space travel and kinetic abilities in space. China's recent space launch schedule has been aggressive, and state funders are looking to pour more subsidies and support for emerging technologies. China's "Made in China" 2025 strategy explicitly calls out ten sectors: next-generation information technology, electric vehicles, machines/robots, energy equipment, aerospace (including space travel), agricultural automation and machinery, high-tech ships, new materials, advanced railways, and biotechnology.

Nowhere was this trend more visible than in Chinese state interactions with censorship, a trend that would conflict with Bitcoin. Under Jiang Zemin's rule, the Internet came to China in 1994. However, there was always fear that the Internet could be used to undermine the party's rule—though a powerful economic tool, its potential for political ramifications has always scared the party.[141] The Ministry of Public Security, throughout the 90s, had been developing a "Golden Shield" project for the Chinese Internet. Conscious of this tension, the political leadership wanted to open up, but do so in a way that was under the state's control. Google was soon banned from the mainland over sensitive political content. The Great Firewall that developed is a centralized version of the Internet, using the state's control and the graphing of digital gatekeepers to the powers a state traditionally wants. It blocks access to certain IP addresses for Chinese users, and allows centralized spoofing of other addresses to redirect users (sometimes without their knowledge) to alternative sites.[142]

How China dealt with the Internet was a preview of how it wants to deal with Bitcoin and cryptocurrencies today. The right amount of openness is the amount that keeps the Chinese Communist Party firmly in control. However, the party has to balance commercial concerns with political ones, as seen in commercial encryption.[143] When national security advocates build backdoors into systems, the ability to encrypt data is critical to keep commercial systems running—and is undermined by those backdoors. China's Encryption Law of 2020 is an explicit acknowledgment of the fact that encryption has long surpassed the ability of the state to control it, yet also offers clues into the government's attempt to try to control everything within its grasp. China's old 1989 regulatory regime for encryption required licenses to produce and sell encryption.[144] It also only permitted domestic encryption standards built in China. The new law is a concession to something the American government (which has much more granular insight and control into international commercial encryption standards—the NSA and NIST, both American government agencies, were involved in creating international encryption primitives) has long conceded: that government controls on encryption would fetter the commercial potential for secure communications, which is foundational for e-commerce, online banking, and more.

Commerce may win in the balance between commerce and national security, but nothing is certain regarding the murky Chinese state. It has established that blockchain is an information standard it wants to dominate. It has convened the National Blockchain and Distributed Accounting Technology Standardization Technical Committee with a smattering of the most prominent Chinese technology firms and representatives of the Chinese state. The China Standards project of 2035 includes an emphasis on blockchain. In a 5-year plan separate from the "Made in China" process (and part of China's standard economic planning), the Chinese party-state placed blockchain in the same place as AI, big data, and cloud computing as a standard that China eventually wants to export around the world.[145]

In practice, however, it means that new projects from state guidance funds, provincial administrations, and efforts convened by the central government will gain precedence, and "blockchain" will be featured throughout its interactions with other software standards and uses. Data and "blockchain" can be expected to integrate with any sector in China's "Made in 2025" plan. For example, blockchain projects to track carbon emissions will carefully track electric vehicles, new materials, and other technologies to address energy costs and efficiency. However, among the closest set of intersections for "blockchain" in the Chinese setting is probably how the data will be used directly in interaction with other software systems and standards China is building. The Chinese state has decided that the best way to spur this forward is to create dedicated servers and resources in remote regions without economic opportunity: a top-down approach to computation and the innovation that will emerge as a result of these efforts rather than a bottom-up perspective that empowers innovators and technologists.

The People's Republic of China has seldom (until recently with Bytedance and TikTok) had global success in exporting its software platforms. As a form of defense, it bans American technology companies such as Google and Facebook from serving domestic markets and bans American-based encryption standards. That defensive posture is what Bitcoin has fallen under. However, this track record may change with the rise of upstarts such as TikTok (owned by ByteDance) and cutting-edge mobile networks on 5G, as well as manufacturing. China is now seeking to play offense by leveraging its capability to manufacture new technologies and assemble standards for the next level of data—from central bank digital currencies to "blockchain" across the world. What drives this appeal is the ability to drive specific, individualized action from the cacophony of communication and data the Internet generates. The Chinese party-state system that combines social credit, data tracking, and the idea of "blockchain" permanence has already been deployed to punish individuals. Social credit is the Chinese party-state's attempt (through provincial standards) to get a better handle on the data out there and provide a ledger on every citizen "under Heaven."

Social Credit

The Chinese party-state can assemble data systems not only to watch and analyze but also to act. A perfect example is figuring out who should get access to the digital yuan and if certain accounts should be given individual-level interest rates or access. What would happen to dissidents, for example, in a state that combined some individualized scoring system with an actionable and individual-level control on finances? Where the "trustworthy will roam under heaven, while the discredited cannot take a single step?"[146] The People's Republic of China is already severely credentialed: the region of a Chinese citizen's birth dictates their economic mobility through the hukou system, purchasing a mobile device means registering their passport with the authorities, and new systems aim to track people throughout their travels through machine learning. What will happen to the Chinese people and the people to whom the Chinese party-state will export this system?

China's broader techno-nationalist stack aims to impose the physical control the party owns into its own version of cyberspace. It's one thing to be able to process data from financial flows to health data. It's another to tabulate each one of these pieces of data and augment each citizen's records with the government's own notes and to create a system that generates as much data as possible about citizens and residents, traps it within the Chinese Communist Party's control, and then uses the party's mentality of broad punishment to deliver overwhelming force.

Social credit in a Chinese setting has already been ridiculed worldwide with memes that lambast it. The general gist is to add an absurd amount of "positive" or "negative" scores according to favorable actions to China. The actual policy is similar to any policy worldwide: messy and incomplete. Interoperable data standards are an issue: localities with specific data standards find it difficult to communicate with one another, which means that even national intent struggles against the roughness of implementing data algorithms across a large enough population. However, it is in its intent and the specific mechanics of Chinese state policy that one can begin indeed tracing out what makes it different—and what makes it play so well (or poorly, depending on your perspective) with new data-focused technologies such as machine learning, or "blockchain."

Named the (roughly translated as social credit score), it is a formal improvement and consolidation of a financial credit score first implemented in the 1980s when Deng Xiaoping moved China to a more pragmatic position on capitalism. Back then, there was a need to bring a poor economy with vast amounts of rural and unbanked populations up to speed with conventional financial credit scoring. The system that evolved was typical of one found in any developed economy—trying to develop some record of an individual's financial trustworthiness based on their interactions with the retail banking system. Soon, however, the party would seek to make it a broader score that could evaluate whether or not the party could trust any individual under its rule.

The social credit system is evolving toward a consolidated credit score portfolio, considering "trust" across different stakeholders and factors. Wen Jiabao, the premier during the Hu Jintao era of leadership that immediately preceded Xi Jinping's reign, announced a more cohesive and comprehensive set of standards in 2014. The Chinese credit system can easily be bent toward party objectives, just like there are apps to command loyalty from party cadres on the Chinese Internet (a foreign concept in many other places). The world has absorbed the American credit system, built on top of a credit score on each citizen it can find and documentation throughout the process of accessing bank reserves. The Chinese system aims to replicate this level of surveillance and incorporate data factors specific to the Chinese party-state's interests. Any additional layer of data or punishment could tip the balance toward dystopia.

China also has a party-focused perspective, a vast array of tools, and an Internet that refuses foreign connections or anonymous devices and makes privacy-preserving technologies like Virtual Private Networks ("VPNs") illegal. The ability to track people's spending throughout the economy strongly indicates their activities and, potentially, their thoughts and ideologies. It offers another layer to this score that the Chinese party-state can unlock by promoting the digital yuan. The financial control that follows (e.g., individualized interest rates for certain people, denial of access to services and goods) is a hyper-accelerated version of the perils of central bank digital currencies—a central bank digital currency with "unique Chinese characteristics." Though China's central bank has claimed it doesn't want to go there, the point is that with the digital yuan they could.

Misconceptions about social credit abound. The large number that sums up all good and bad actions does not quite exist; instead, a set of standards to be implemented across the Chinese party-state and tending toward total surveillance is being built. The social credit system can be concerning and fraught with peril even if it isn't quite yet the Black Mirror system memes and pundits paint it as: a running tabulation, run by private companies, that follows precisely from the ratings of people around you. But perhaps its full implementation will be many times worse.[147]

The Chinese party-state works through its organs in each county and province to set standards. An English version of Guangdong province's social credit regulations is close to the norm. There is an emphasis on creditworthiness and also pursuing accountability for untrustworthy activities.[148] Unlike American credit systems, however, the definitions here go beyond just economic accountability and the ability to track debt payments. There is a reference to ethics, family values, and personal character—a broader accounting for credit that can include loyalty to the party and other traits most would not associate with social standing. The national standards passed down to provinces aim to reduce anonymity to almost nothing, making it impractical to be online without divulging your real physical identity. The rules are layered with references to personal responsibility, disregarding even the corporate shield (i.e., if you own a company that falls afoul of certain laws or regulations, then you will personally suffer). The punishments can be broad and have nothing to directly do with underlying action. While provincial standards differ, sometimes significantly, they all include an element of negative actions being recorded and used as enforcement against companies and individuals. If someone accumulates too many negative actions, the state will act differently—it will make reviews harder and seek to punish the individual. Though these standards and intentions are more theory than practice in many cases, the intent is clear, and the technology is largely there.[149]

The social credit system also seems to be an effort to allow markets to operate but to keep core functions tightly under the control of the socialist party-state—following a similar example of transitioning from Alipay and WeChat Pay to a central bank digital currency. Private systems like Alibaba's Sesame Credit have been denied access to launch pilot programs for private credit score investigation companies—the same sign of mistrust on fundamental national security issues the Chinese party-state seems to convey with the digital yuan, potentially hedging against private payment processors. The techno-nationalist system being created already has legs, with the social credit score providing a theory and purpose, while the underlying legs of data collection, from the digital yuan to DNA collection, make it almost impossible to escape a system firmly under the control of the Chinese party-state.

Individual Consequences for a Social System

The stories that have come out of China's use of data to punish dissidents are instructive for a future with the techno-nationalist system. The most tangible example of the social credit system is how it operates with blacklists. Anybody who loses a final court judgment against themselves will suddenly find an array of forces placed against them along with onerous restrictions. They are forbidden from purchasing certain goods and services, including airplane tickets that might help them escape from this situation. In 2018, this meant that the Chinese party-state denied access 17.5 million times to those looking to buy flights, and 5.5 million times for buyers of train tickets in order to get them to comply with the blacklists and pay back debts these Chinese nationals might have owed.[150] China has always had this layer of control, but by putting it into provincial standards, the party is more coordinated internally, and this level of standardization and control allows for easier export to other willing countries deciding how they want to position themselves with the Internet.

These examples get more pressing as the Chinese party-state confronts "states of exception." Legal scholars in China have gravitated to the German philosopher Carl Schmitt, who was a philosopher who joined the Nazi Party and who helped Hitler form the intellectual basis for the fascist German state. Major academic databases are filled with hundreds of references to his scholarship.[151] The phenomenon of "Schmitt fever" doesn't just rest in academia. In Hong Kong's "Constitution Day Seminar," Peking University law professor Chen Duanhong lectured about Schmittian concepts to the Hong Kong government—which had just finished implementing a National Security Law that would imprison political leaders, journalists, and more.[152] In Carl Schmitt's "state of exception," an abnormal situation confronts the state, which must decide then to suspend all legal norms and to accord power to a sovereign that can effectively navigate the polity through the chaos it faces.[153] In modern-day China, this is a direct reference to Xi Jinping.

Three states of exception have reigned prominently, from Hong Kong to COVID-19 to Xinjiang/Tibet. In these states of exception, the level of punishment and technological tracking have seen very few (if any) restraints– and the techno-nationalist surveillance state built on top of the standards of the social credit score has been enacted to terrifying effect. From late 2016, the Chinese party-state has subjected members of the Uyghur ethnic minority to mass detention and a surveillance apparatus that tracks their movements and behaviors. They have linked everything from the color of cars to physical height to the national identity card of many residents of Xinjiang—creating a database with tragic implications. Some who fall afoul of the standards are detained arbitrarily. Use of encrypted privacy-protecting technologies is seen as suspicious from the outset and can cause one to fall into being watched by the authorities—with potential consequences to follow.[154] For example, in Xinjiang an imam left, and because of this his daughter was imprisoned in a camp. Another Muslim man was beaten and interrogated and then placed in a detention camp—after being told that WhatsApp was illegal. Still another had local authorities tell him to stop complaining through a family member in China after he posted videos asking why his aunt had been detained for seemingly no reason.[155] During COVID-19, Chinese state authorities turned the health tracking app forced on every Chinese resident to detect and trace COVID-19 cases "red" for potential protesters of a large financial scandal that left people deprived of their savings.[156] The techno-nationalist stack China is implementing may seem theoretical, but it has had a tangible impact on many individuals who have been deprived of their freedoms—including their life savings, stuck and frozen in a Chinese financial system that serves as a cog in a greater system of control.

Social credit score standards intersect with certain technological buzzwords in their implementation in creating a full techno-nationalist stack. Big data, blockchain, cloud computing, and artificial intelligence are encouraged for use by the party-state—showing that the leapfrog technologies the Chinese party-state is assembling supports its intent to control cyberspace and physical space. This is augmented by Chinese state directives that ensure "real" state-issued IDs are needed to access phone numbers and other critical services. Add to that the stark number of physical cameras, location-based device tracking, and facial recognition employed to track physical movement—even DNA collection.[157] The Chinese party-state wants the ability to "judge the trustworthy" and not have to rely on private intermediaries to do this core state function.

Its rapid and comprehensive action and punitive nature will mean that China's techno-nationalist stack will grow better at targeting people with more data. This offers a path to take the chaos of the Internet and personal self-expression into the claws of state repression—opening the door to a world where anybody's digital expression can be added to their identity and punished at scale by the states they live in. In China the goal is to assemble a list of the "seriously untrustworthy" based on their social credit score. Punishable "crimes" can range widely, but one that stands out is assembling in order to disrupt social order. Protests in Shanghai that broke out against onerous COVID restrictions would have likely seen each protester be added to such a blacklist.

Conclusion: China's Endgame on Dissent

By criminalizing dissent against the party-state and establishing a technological record and system that scales to the millions of people under its control, the Chinese party-state aims to make its control permanent by embedding it within technological innovations. China wants to expand its influence by proving that it can develop into a world-leading economy and maintain its position without the need for democracy or many individual freedoms. The playbook is based on technological development, using its strength in manufacturing and an attempt at an indigenous Internet and data systems to find the balance between giving entrepreneurs enough freedom and profit to help grow the economy while firmly keeping China under party-state control. If China is successful at doing this and incorporating a central bank digital currency while warding off Bitcoin, the open Internet, privacy-preserving technologies, and adjacent "freedom-tech" that helps people openly communicate with one another will fall under attack, and the Chinese playbook will be an appealing prospect to any authoritarian who wants to build wealth and an independent tax base while maintaining absolute political control.

It is clear that what is happening within the People's Republic of China now matters throughout the rest of the world. The world's second-largest economic power may become the world's largest economy in our lifetimes. The gravity it will pull will affect the world around China— the People's Republic of China will not only set its standards for political control through technology and a state-driven model of technical development, but it will also seek to export these standards around the world. The question being asked is whether people will accept being controlled so completely by their states. How people and nation-states respond to this drive will shape the 21st century—and beyond.

Chapter Eight
Three Paths Forward

The battle between Bitcoin and China for the future will expand internationally to every country worldwide. China's attempts to set international standards for central bank digital currencies and export the techno-nationalist tech stack is part of a broader international fight over what will win: technology that empowers people to be free or empowers states to rule their peoples.

There are three paths nation-states can take: one is to try to repress open-source technologies and to try to ban their use, like China. The second is to embrace Bitcoin as a monetary standard and elevate it to legal tender, or otherwise be more receptive to Bitcoin and open-source technologies like El Salvador. Finally, there is the squishy middle, where most states currently are trying to regulate Bitcoin and its many applications, but not going over the line to outright ban mining and exchanges.

The Roots of the Battle

This battle has its roots in the first "crypto wars," fought over the ability to export open-source cryptography worldwide, many of whose primitives are now deeply rooted in Bitcoin. It was through export controls that the first "crypto wars" were fought, as cryptographers trying to publish their research in open-access journals with international audiences were threatened with prosecution.[158] Public key cryptography now plays a crucial role in securing the modern Internet, allowing people to communicate and transact with one another easily. It is the underpinning of modern commerce and is largely taken for granted. As a result, many people on the Internet today declare the "first crypto" wars won.

The cypherpunks that created the core around Satoshi's creation came of age during this era—inherently skeptical of the government's drive to crack down on new technologies, they vowed to "publish their code" and make "networks safe for privacy."[159] They were coders and thinkers born of the rough shards of the early Internet: the early hackers, builders, and tricksters of the connective sinew of the Internet that would soon engulf the world. Some of those early cypherpunks would later become part of the early core of Bitcoin's creators.

Hal Finney, who would later go on to be the second transactor in Bitcoin after Satoshi, was on the cypherpunks mailing list and would take the time in the 1990s to collaborate with Phil Zimmerman to build PGP (pretty good privacy), allowing people to hash and unhash their messages using public key cryptography. To this day this technique is still in use for those who want to send secure messages over what are assumed to be insecure channels. Adam Back came up with a rough concept for "proof-of-work" on the newsletter, and Wei Dai and Nick Szabo both came up with differing versions as part of the Cypherpunk lists of digital money: b-money and BitGold. The cypherpunks realized they needed something like Bitcoin, which would take public key encryption and proof-of-work and implement them in a distributed fashion to create money that the banking system couldn't censor for an Internet that was hard for governments to control.

Though export controls faded in terms of a legal threat—a federal court case eventually ruled that code was protected speech and that government prohibitions on code should be strictly prohibited[160]—national security forces are still looking to undermine encryption. The "second crypto war" has also found its target in Bitcoin. Central banks have commissioned research to show that Bitcoin increases volatility in their domestic money supply. Stakeholders in the conventional banking system have leveled fierce criticism of the environmental effects of Bitcoin and the "criminal" implications of its usage. States are using analysis firms such as Chainalysis to crack the pseudonymous nature of Bitcoin and make sense of all of the transactions happening on the public chain, even if they are not states that have partially or completed banning transacting in Bitcoin. The Department of Justice has gone after modern-day cypherpunks such as Virgil Griffith for "sharing information about" cryptocurrencies to the North Koreans—a harkening back to the export controls of yore.[161]

However, the leading proponent of cross-border repression of Bitcoin is China, which as the world's largest economic power has tried its hardest to reduce or even eliminate the use of Bitcoin in the physical territory it controls. This split is not a simple China versus Bitcoin war and a simple freedom versus repression theme, but a nuanced panoply of how nation-states in different conditions will deal with this new open-source technology.

Attempting control doesn't just stop at financial bits and bytes and Bitcoin, but applies to any information humans can send to one another online. Authoritarian governments worldwide are looking to the Chinese Internet as a model for how they can benefit from the commercial implications of being connected to the Internet while managing the communications and connections between their people. Under the label of "cyber sovereignty," the People's Republic of China has tried to get other states to try to import its level of control over their domestic Internet by getting them to uphold centralized control while trying to dissuade "foreign" influence.[162] China also offers to support certain technical implementations that are versions of its "Great Firewall" technologies. Blocking technologies across Russia and the Middle East have been used, with the Chinese state providing both technological tools and large-scale training of foreign officials. National security forces and a coalition of stakeholders in "free" countries also seek to undermine the ability of people to communicate using end-to-end encryption and want to moderate the content placed on social media platforms.

For simplification and classification, there are three broad paths nation-states have taken or can take, keeping in mind that each nation-state has a rich history with Bitcoin and the Internet. The Chinese model of (attempted) censorship is a potential inspiration for some countries, while El Salvador's open embrace of Bitcoin might inspire others, with a majority of countries remaining in the comfortable middle.

The first model, emulating the Chinese approach, involves active law enforcement to slow down Bitcoin adoption. The second and opposite model, broadly defined as acceptance and endorsement of Bitcoin, uses state infrastructure to build applications for the Bitcoin ecosystem, such as localized wallets and perhaps the enforcement or encouragement of Bitcoin as legal tender within a country—the most prominent case so far being El Salvador. The third model is a sort of "strategic ambiguity"—recognizing that Bitcoin is a payment system that some citizens will use but which does not advance strong points of view on anything beyond policy papers studying energy effects and how Bitcoin fits into current financial system regulations (e.g., Know Your Customer and anti-money laundering regulation).

The Techno-Authoritarians

Players: Bangladesh, Venezuela, Bolivia, Iran, North Korea, Bolivia, Nigeria, Turkey

Typical approach: Trade in Bitcoin is banned and the governments in question typically take a techno-nationalist approach around the Internet. Some of these countries are also most aggressive at piloting a central bank digital currency. This is aligned with China's approach to Bitcoin, and is the approach China is looking to spread and model.

Most countries in the world do not have the economic gravitas or techno-nationalist focus like China does. They take their cues from China regarding Bitcoin and technological development, especially those that are outsiders to the American financial order. This leads some economic outsiders closest to the Chinese world order to seem friendly to Bitcoin to shore up their potential survival better—yet turning around and using authoritarian technology on their own people. Other countries react similarly to the Chinese model because of their interests and authoritarian tendencies, even if they are not fully aligned with China.

Bangladesh is one of the strictest countries in the world regarding Bitcoin. Ownership and transacting in virtual currencies is forbidden. Bangladesh also bans Bitcoin mining. The main concern from Bangladesh's central bank is related to "terrorist funding" and "money laundering." Punishment of up to 12 years can happen for people merely transacting in cryptocurrencies like Bitcoin. Bangladesh is also edging close to China's sphere of influence.

Ever since the reign of Hugo Chavez, Venezuela has been an avowed ideological enemy of the United States. Under Maduro, the country has continued its trend of domestic political repression as well as being increasingly cut off from the international financial system. As a result, it has ironically been at the forefront of new digital fashions of transacting. It tried to ICO a cryptocurrency known as Petro, which was supposed to be backed by either gold or the ample oil reserves Venezuela usually relies on for its economy. However, the cryptocurrency failed; it was not available on most cryptocurrency exchanges and barely got any traction. The Venezuelan state has moved on to a central bank digital currency, and the Venezuelan military has seized many Bitcoin mining machines.[163] Meanwhile, the Chinese state has grown in terms of its trade with Venezuela and is now Venezuela's second-largest trading partner. Maduro and the Venezuelan leadership have signaled a desire to supply China and Russia with more oil "rain or shine."

Since 2014, the Bolivian central bank has banned the use of Bitcoin—only a year or so after China issued a regulatory notice on Bitcoin. The reasoning is that no currency other than the one issued by the central bank should be valid in Bolivia's territory—matching China's worst fears about the substitution of Bitcoin as currency.

Iran has been cut off from the international economic system and sanctioned heavily by the United States. This has been a death knell for an economy reliant on oil exports. As a result, Iran has sometimes embraced Bitcoin, licencing and allowing specific categories of Bitcoin miners. It has allowed the use of cryptocurrencies to pay for imports.[164] However, the Iranian state has detained "house" miners who are mining outside of the government's embrace, and it has also decided to ban Bitcoin miners on a seasonal basis.

Nigeria was one of the first countries to implement a central bank digital currency, trying to create a cashless society through legal restrictions on paper cash—something that has already led to protests nationwide due to concerns about financial privacy and security.[165] Nigeria's central bank gave restrictions for cash withdrawals as it tried to starve out the paper money it once maintained and get a firmer grasp on the large informal economy in Nigeria. The IMF put it as a positive for the naira in terms of financial inclusion and untangling the informal economy.[166] Toward the end of the paper, the IMF says they stand ready to promote examples of eNaira usage for other countries—a digital currency named closely to the e-CNY promoted by China's central bank.

Turkey has a mixed relationship with Bitcoin, but tends

toward the camp of jailing cryptocurrency exchange founders. Erdogan, Turkey's leader, also has a similar philosophy to "blockchain" and Bitcoin as the Chinese party-state, pushing Turkey to be a "producer" of digital assets but warning the Turkish people against "gambling" with cryptocurrencies. Despite the central bank's ban on exchanging goods and services with cryptocurrency, there appears to be considerable bottom-up demand for Bitcoin.

What these countries have in common with China is that despite a top-down approach to trying to keep Bitcoin out of their citizens' hands, there is still significant bottom-up demand from their people, who can navigate these restrictions to trade with one another. For example, even compared to other economies suffering hyperinflation (such as Argentina), Venezuelans use peer-to-peer Bitcoin solutions to transact economic activity; they are the most significant users of the peer-to-peer component of Bitcoin. Local marketplaces show that Venezuela has a high degree of Bitcoin usage on marketplaces such as LocalBitcoins and Paxful (before it left the country).[167]

The people of Iran are using Bitcoin as well. A survey of Bitcoiners on Persian Telegram revealed that individuals were earning critical income through either trading or mining cryptocurrencies, with 25 percent making between $500 and $3,000.[168] There was a high degree of interest in this group in learning more about mining, showing that in oppressive settings, individuals within a nation-state can have independent thoughts about how they can earn their incomes and economic freedoms, and Bitcoin can help in this regard.

Nigeria has long been a place where inflation has made it difficult to do things. Inflation in 1995 touched slightly above 72% in a year, and almost every year brings some weakening of the Nigerian naira.[169] Amid protests against police brutality (#EndSars), the Nigerian government fired upon their people. One of the organizing groups, the Feminist Coalition, started raising funds for protests in Bitcoin to continue. Centralized payment services such as Flutterwave froze funds intended for the protest due to government influence. The balance in Nigeria is being set where individuals and civil society actors are getting used to using Bitcoin.

The Turkish lira is undergoing significant inflation, creating weakness for Erdogan and political leadership across the country. Merchants openly take Tether through Binance and offer lira for trade, allowing people to access the Turkish economy through Bitcoin. An unpredictable lira and weaker domestic currency means that Turkish citizens were looking for goods like gold and other currencies like the United States dollar to hold their earning power. They can "take risks easily," extending well into Bitcoin.[170] Turkish crypto exchange Paribu claimed 8 million Turkish cryptocurrency users in 2022. Ads for Paribu and other cryptocurrency exchanges line the airport and streets of Istanbul.

The Most Bitcoin-Friendly

Players: El Salvador, Central African Republic, Ukraine, Island Nations, Germany, South Korea

The most Bitcoin-friendly countries tend to be those that favor Bitcoin adoption. Exchanges often settle here due to the more relaxed regulatory nature, afraid that settling too close to the United States might invite their founders to unwanted scrutiny, or there are important cultural and governmental reasons for it to be a Bitcoin hub. The most prominent examples are the two governments that as of 2024 have embraced Bitcoin as legal tender and actively built Bitcoin infrastructure for themselves. These are the countries that categorically reject the Chinese-based model of technological repression—though ironically, some of these countries hold close ties to China.

El Salvador is the first nation-state to embrace Bitcoin as legal tender. it is stuck between the US dollar economy it has built itself on and funds from the Chinese party-state for everything from a stadium to water infrastructure. In terms of the US-China dynamic, it is clear that El Salvador is in the middle. Outwardly, its use of Bitcoin is a way for their political leadership to say that El Salvador is a Bitcoin-driven land. It starts with the current leader of El Salvador, Nayib Bukele, who has tried to take the mantle of a Bitcoin nation-state leader. Speaking about Bitcoin and inviting Bitcoin advisors to talk with him, El Salvador has embarked on the most serious nation-state attempt to onboard onto Bitcoin, including creating an "official" wallet for Bitcoin called Chivo.

The case of El Salvador is an interesting one. A dollarized economy that grew out of the conservative right's desire to integrate with the giant American economy to the north more closely now moves toward accepting and mandating Bitcoin as a legal currency. The current party, an offshoot of the conservative El Salvadorian right but a "third party" that claims neither right nor left, is headed by Nayib Bukele. Although from the outside it seems like he is playing the role of a Bitcoin HODLer with a big social media following (participating in Twitter Spaces and parts of Bitcoin culture such as laser eyes) and with the state treasury behind him, El Salvador's pivot to using Bitcoin is more than it seems at first glance. Bukele has been at pains to say that Bitcoin will not replace the dollar anytime soon. However, it is clear that Trump-era sanctions (continued under the Biden Administration), partially motivated by his country's shift to recognizing the People's Republic of China over Taiwan, have eroded his faith in the United States. His English tweets will often resonate with the latest Bitcoin humor or memes—yet his Spanish tweets often reference admiration for Chinese state funding for stadiums and other infrastructure and barely-veiled anger at American financial sanctions.

Bukele's actions speak to the two-bladed nature of Bitcoin: preventing a fully scaled national digital currency from being adopted by a nation-state like El Salvador but also eroding the current financial system upon which the United States drives its hegemony. El Salvador is where these two empires meet: where a boisterous ideologically driven leader can speak about the United States as a "rival" in Spanish that puts El Salvador on sanction lists while speaking of China as a friend for, among other things, funding a stadium—all while tweeting "HODL" memes.

How did this happen? An autonomous zone called El Zonte, a surfing paradise, became known as "Bitcoin Beach" after merchants and users adopted Bitcoin en masse. By leveraging Bitcoin and the Lightning Network, it attracted and rallied people across the Bitcoin ecosystem to El Zonte. What started as a Twitter thread asking for funds quickly became an area that innovated in Bitcoin payments and accepted Lightning throughout the zone. It became a significant reason for the first nation-state to adopt it as a legal tender and build its infrastructure.

When El Salvador first adopted the US dollar as the default currency in its economy, some of it must have been due to the incredible amount of economic activity between the United States and El Salvador. A large number of people from El Salvador have fled the country and landed in the United States after a devastating civil war—sending remittances back home to El Salvador has tied together the American economy with El Salvador even tighter than just through proximity. In 2016, remittances made up 17% of El Salvador's GDP.

However, the dollarization of El Salvador's economy left an uneasy legacy. One survey showed that 62% of the population thought that dollarization was damaging—mainly because El Salvador has yet to see the promised amount of economic growth that the country claimed was the reason for adopting the dollar in the first place. When that growth did not materialize, the United States dollar started having unforeseen consequences for the country. For example, when interest-rate targeting was set toward zero when the United States was trying to revive its economy after the 2008 financial crisis), the El Salvadorian people felt like they got a raw deal.

Bitcoin allows for both a first-mover advantage and some of the benefits El Salvador was trying to capture in the first place with the United States dollar. El Salvador wants to benefit from the attention of the thinkers, technologists, and entrepreneurs associated with Bitcoin and become a hub for remote-friendly tech workers. The ability to hedge economic growth without relying entirely on the will of a central bank miles away benefits countries like El Salvador, who drive toward nation-state adoption of Bitcoin.

However, the story of how El Salvador is looking to grow is more complex than this narrative of Bitcoin versus USD. For one thing, de-dollarization is not comfortably on the table. Bukele's alliance draws many members from the ARENA party grouping that regards the dollarization of El Salvador's economy as a critical part of its political legacy. Bukele has mentioned several times how he is not trying to de-dollarize the economy—Bitcoin is still one form of legal tender, with the USD being another. While the IMF and the United States-led financial world order have come after him with sanctions and other items, it is not like Bitcoin will cause a divorce between El Salvador and the American trade order.

It was quite a surprise when the Central African Republic, the second country to adopt Bitcoin for legal tender, announced its support for Bitcoin. The country does not have Internet access for most of its citizens, and it is one of the poorest economies in the world. The country ranks second-last as of 2022 on the Human Development Index, in front of only Niger. However, this story also shows the romantic possibilities of countries adopting a Bitcoin standard. The Central African Republic wants to change its current condition. It has a political class questioning its current monetary system based on the Central African Franc, a legacy of the French colonial system that once reigned throughout most of Western and Central Africa. China's relationship with the Central African Republic helps add another element to this discussion. Like El Salvador,

China is cultivating a positive relationship through training and investments. The Chinese government has, for example, constructed a 20,000-person stadium, similar to the funding of the national stadium in El Salvador.

It might seem that the Central African Republic is trying to hedge against its former colonial master in trying to find a way to distance itself from the overwhelming monetary hegemony placed on it without openly drawing the complete ire of the European Union. It is also somewhat distanced from the United States, which had shut down its embassy in 2012 due to rising violence and concerns about the political framework in the Central African Republic. However, in truth, this action of embracing Bitcoin as legal tender helps elevate the world's second-least developed country. In the global battle for geopolitical attention, the Central African Republic has won very few of those battles. By embracing Bitcoin, the Central African Republic has ensured it is more than a footnote in France's ledgers and more than just one target among many of China's investments.

Ukraine is in an odd geopolitical position. With strong economic ties to China, Ukraine has been ideally placed as a "bridge" between West and East, at least when it comes to the minds of Chinese state planners. However, China has also declared a partnership with "no limits" when it comes to Russia—a country that has invaded Ukraine and committed countless atrocities. Dependent on Western military alliances for funding and support, Ukraine is now close enough to the West to bear the brunt of Chinese censors but not close enough for a no-fly zone or direct military intervention from NATO. Perhaps unique among every nation in this chapter, it is the one most under fire for its "alignment" status, with Russian officials holding that condition over Ukraine in return for a ceasefire to the war.

Stuck between these two worlds, Ukraine will have to find its place in the middle geopolitically—a challenging task to do under normal circumstances, never mind a full-throttled and bloody war.

For some individuals stuck in warfare, there is no choice: bank reserves are hard to port across borders. Ukrainians might have had access to domestic reserves and a bank account, but that is no guarantee that they can bring their savings with them, especially during war. Ukraine was a country that showed high Bitcoin usage patterns even before the Russian invasion. A study by Merchant Marine found that by combining the number of owners of Bitcoin, businesses that accept Bitcoin, and the number of Bitcoin ATMs physically present, the three factors meant that Ukraine was estimated to have the second-highest Bitcoin usage in the world (behind the United States). The Ukrainian state has used Bitcoin as a fundraising mechanism for resisting the Russian invasion, helping to raise millions of dollars into cryptocurrency wallets and actively soliciting donations in Bitcoin. For now, Ukraine is in the middle of bloodshed and war. It can be trite to talk about economic matters when people are facing death daily, though Bitcoin has played a role for people trying to escape the chaos, confusion, and bloodshed.

The Caribbean islands also offer a unique spot to drive Bitcoin adoption. Their closeness to the United States and their reputation for financial flows and tourism have led to eight live implementations of central bank digital currencies, including the Sand Dollar of the Bahamas, launched in 2019 with the claim that (at the time) it was the world's first actual fully scaled central bank digital currency. As of May 2023, the Caribbean has eight of the nine live central bank digital currencies worldwide, with Nigeria rounding out the list. They were also more friendly to cryptocurrency exchanges such as FTX.

On the other side of the world, the Pacific Islands offer a similar story. The Marshall Islands is tiny from a population standpoint relative to other nation-states. The 2018 census counted around 60,000 people living in the country. Settled by Micronesians who migrated there by canoe, the chain of islands in the Pacific Ocean has glorious beaches and natural resources abounding. The Marshall Islands are a parliamentary republic with an executive presidency and deep integration with the United States economy. The Marshall Islands are at a scale where more significant federal services are provided by the United States, including protection from the United States military. Aid from the United States is what powers most of the economy in the Marshall Islands. Nevertheless, similar to El Salvador, the country sought to hedge that by creating another domestic currency—a national "cryptocurrency" that went through the ICO process. Though this was done on another chain rather than Bitcoin itself, it shows a theme that has been present when it comes to Bitcoin adoption: economies that are overly dependent on American financial aid or economic inputs looking to chart their path in the world.

Germany occupies a truly interesting perch on the world's Internet. Tor is a network of nodes that pass users' Internet traffic amongst themselves, making it harder to see where or what any particular Internet user using a Tor browser is doing. In many respects, it is a network that shares similarities with Bitcoin: network access depends on the uptime of nodes provided by those who believe in the system. The code is open source, and anybody can tinker with it. Technologies such as Wasabi Wallet incorporate Tor usage to preserve privacy for Bitcoin users. Because of the density of hosting nodes for technologies like Tor, parts of Germany (most prominently the Kreuzberg district of Berlin) have been associated with an innovative hacker culture. There are Bitcoin-related and Lightning-related hackathons in the area, which help Germany maintain a unique position regarding peer-to-peer-driven Internet protocols.

Germany is a country that has subsequently recognized early on that Bitcoin is a form of money—a unit of account that people use to transact with one another. The government accepts various forms of cryptocurrency payments. It has generally taken a relatively lenient line on Bitcoin, even among the Western countries that impose a semi-form of control on it. One example is that Bitcoin held for longer than a year is not subject to capital gains in Germany, and those who transact in Bitcoin in Germany do not need to pay VAT (sales tax) on those particular items. In effect, Germany treats Bitcoin more like a currency than its traditional financial allies in the West. Though it is not recognized as coming from any government, it is regarded as a legitimate way to pay and a currency of its own to a certain extent.

The European Union as a whole, however, is significantly less friendly—and has advanced a policy paper that asks member states to track "crypto-mining" activity and energy usage. Since the EU is currently shutting down the industry and prioritizing residences in the energy crisis, it can be easy to see Bitcoin mining as an easy activity for authorities to condemn and try to shut down, as the People's Republic of China has.

South Korea has been a cryptocurrency hotspot—its exchanges typically trade at the highest fiat amount premiums for Bitcoin. In the recent presidential election, both candidates advanced pro-cryptocurrency positions. As one of the Asian Tigers, South Korea has both developed economically, with Samsung as a critical economic and semiconductor force, as well as gradually integrated itself deeply into the American financial order. It is now a stalwart ally, counted upon to defuse North Korean tensions and to be part of a bloc of countries that can counter the People's Republic of China.

South Korea has moved to regulate, tax, and investigate cryptocurrency exchanges, which have become a significant player in the Korean economy. After the collapse of LUNA (a purported "stablecoin"), local authorities asked for information about stablecoins, showing how concerned they were about the effect of Bitcoin and cryptocurrencies on the local economy. They eventually issued a red notice for Do Kwan, the founder of LUNA, and tried to pursue him across international borders.

Bitcoin trading has an outsize effect in South Korea. In one day, 21% of the trading volume in Bitcoin was between Korean-tied accounts. It tends to be the third-largest trading region behind Japan and the United States. At first glance, South Koreans are very interested in the price action rather than the fundamentals of the network. South Korea's history is fascinating to consider in this context:

once a nation bent by poverty and war, it is just generations away from being deemed the "impossible nation"—and the looming specter of its neighbor to the north, always ready to threaten missile strikes, may keep that threat fresh for most South Koreans.

The Middle Ground

Players: The United States and its core "Five Eyes" allies (UK, Canada, Australia, and New Zealand), Taiwan, Greece, Kenya, Mexico

The middle-ground approach involves little to no bans on Bitcoin usage. Bitcoin isn't banned, and most of these countries largely revolve around the American tech stack and "global" Internet. The most common way to try to control Bitcoin is to restrict access to exchanges and to implement a mining ban. The countries here tend to follow the United States, where Bitcoin has no official advantage. The approach is toward regulating the use of Bitcoin through the financial system by attaching Know Your Customer/Anti-Money Laundering restrictions so that there can't be anonymous payments and financial information flows to the banks and regulatory authorities the United States uses to monitor world financial flows. Perhaps a good proxy for the nations in this group is that their central bank will warn that Bitcoin isn't a recognized currency, and they may even not authorize their domestic banking system to work with Bitcoin—yet other regulatory agencies don't ban outright the availability of exchanges and/or look at Bitcoin mining bans.

The United States is a mixed environment for Bitcoin. There are representatives of Congress that are strongly pro-Bitcoin, and they come from across the political left and political right: a rare bipartisan sight. There is a Congressional Blockchain Conference within the halls of Congress, composed of both Democrats and Republicans. Partly as a result, Bitcoin has never been banned in the United States in a way that we have seen with China. Local politicians like the Mayor of Miami have embraced it as a way to get tech jobs and revitalize their city as "startup hubs." However, former presidential candidate Ron Desantis said he would support Bitcoin and ban the use of central bank digital currencies if elected. A raft of other politicians have talked about a central bank digital currency ban, from presidential candidate Robert F. Kennedy Jr. to Senator Cruz from Texas. There are some politicians that go out of their way to express pro-Bitcoin views, like Senator Lummis from Wyoming. Some policymakers deride Bitcoin's environmental effect and would likely want some level of "regulation" to be put on the network, including prominent critics such as Senator Elizabeth Warren, who once said that Bitcoin "puts the system at the whims of some shadowy faceless group of super coders and miners, which does not sound better to me." In a country where the "shadow banking system" received much of the blame for the 2008 financial meltdown, those amount to fighting words.

However, there are no exchange bans in the United States on a federal level. The CFTC regulates Bitcoin—it is not regarded as a currency, so the Federal Reserve does not directly oversee it. However, the CFTC is only concerned with derivatives regulation and does not directly regulate Bitcoin on a cash basis as a commodity. The former chair of the CFTC has opined that the industry needs an SRO, or a self-regulatory organization such as FINRA, for Bitcoin and cryptocurrency as a whole. There are multiple competing executive agencies here, with some backing off because there is enough decentralization such that there is no jurisdiction for them so far (the SEC), while others are aggressively stepping into the space to stake their ground (the IRS, which has multiple rules on the taxation of digital assets).

Timothy Massad, the former head of the CFTC, summed up the overarching attitude: "I think people still want to see what the US does and follow us." The American model remains a reference for an American-dominated international financial and trade order. However, he also remarked that he "thinks we should be moving faster." Developments in China and Hong Kong, especially the recent loosening around cryptocurrency rules in the latter, are driving the conversation rather than the United States. The United States may have approved spot Bitcoin ETFs, but Hong Kong is thinking about offering ETFs that allow withdrawals in Bitcoin. There are no mining bans on a federal level. However, some states (such as New York state) are considering implementing bans on a state level due to the "carbon emissions" and environmental costs they associate with Bitcoin mining. The ability to run Bitcoin nodes and to contribute to the network in that way is the element of Bitcoin that, as of the early 2020s, was on the surest footing: code is protected speech under the First Amendment. While the Federal Reserve and Congress have studied a "digital dollar," it is not something that is being piloted or prioritized in a way that the digital yuan has been airdropped into production. The United States seems very much behind when it comes to central bank digital currencies—perhaps a uniquely good thing in a world that should be skeptical about global standards for central bank digital currency—but perhaps a bad sign for those who want to ensure that China does not maintain its early lead in setting standards here.

Still, there is law enforcement movement on Bitcoin, with the United States leveraging its place as "financial world cop" to go after Bitcoin stakeholders. American regulators have gone after some exchanges like Bitmex for not obeying the Bank Secrecy Act (BSA), the centerpiece of the KYC-AML (know your customer, anti-money laundering) regime. There have been sanctions put on decentralized protocols, which have made their code on Github dormant. The United States government is also actively engaged in litigation against Binance and FTX.

Australia's relationship with Bitcoin is similar to those of the other ANZAC nations. The largest exchange is CoinSpot, which offers 400+ trading pairs of cryptocurrencies and Bitcoin. It is legal for Australian citizens to hold Bitcoin and to purchase it. However, like some other countries in ANZAC, banks are skittish about people making transactions and purchasing Bitcoin, and there have been outright bans on transactions going to Bitcoin exchanges.[171]

New Zealand is considering a central bank digital currency. It will be heavily influenced by the e-CNY's design. However, it is facing some competition, with Chinese-originated exchanges such as Huobi propping up and obtaining licenses in New Zealand, a more fertile place to ply its trade than in its native homeland due to New Zealand's middle-ground approach. Perhaps the most notable blip in New Zealand's relationship with Bitcoin has been the hack of Cryptopia, an exchange that lost millions in user funds.

To the north of its giant neighbor, Canada always feels the trembles of what happens in the United States, just like a mouse sleeping with an "elephant." In invoking the Emergencies Act and censoring access to bank accounts and financial flows to support the "Truckers" convoy, Canada has shown a playbook for incorporating Bitcoin into broader state repression.

Since the United Kingdom and the city of London offer themselves up as financial hubs, it can be easy to see London becoming a European center for innovations like Bitcoin. Measured by the number of Bitcoin transactions, the estimated number of Bitcoin owners, and the number of Bitcoin ATMs present, the United Kingdom is also ranked high with regard to Bitcoin usage. All of the ANZAC countries have unique aspects to their relationship with China—but their stances can expect to harden and they will likely take the American lead on everything from China policy to Bitcoin.

As of July 23rd, 2022, Taiwan's Financial Supervisory Commission (FSC) (a rough equivalent to the SEC in the United States) has tried to implement a ban on buying cryptocurrencies with credit cards—a sign that Taiwan is not very friendly to cryptocurrencies, though not as outright hostile as China. Taiwan's current Digital Minister, Audrey Tang, drew a contract from Apple that paid in Bitcoin, meaning there is some interest at Taiwan's highest level of governance.[172] As the semiconductor manufacturing hub of the world, with TSMC projected to build the most sophisticated chips, Taiwan also has an outsized role in Bitcoin mining and protecting the network. Bitmain, one of the leading producers of cutting-edge miners, has orders out for the most sophisticated 5-nanometer chips. Given that TSMC decided on a limited range of partners to scale this new technology with, it must have been a choice to include one of the world's preeminent Bitcoin mining manufacturers to have early access. However, Bitmain and Taiwan have had a contentious relationship at times, with the Taiwanese state investigating the mining manufacturer for the accusation that it was illegally setting up shell companies to recruit Taiwanese semiconductor engineers to help its chip-making advances.

As of May 31st, 2022, Kenya is part of a wave of African central banks acting in concert across the continent to raise the target interest rate to try to forestall inflationary pressures.[173] It is also a country set to suffer through demand for the US dollar: manufacturers are clamoring for US dollars even as Kenya's central bank denies a shortage.[174] There is no legal restriction against trading or buying Bitcoin, though Kenya's central bank has discouraged Kenyan citizens from purchasing any Bitcoin. However, this has not stopped community activity and Bitcoin adoption, with Paxful, a peer-to-peer Bitcoin trading platform, reporting that millions of US dollars' worth of value in Bitcoin was being transacted in Kenya. This interest can be seen in the high Google trends rate for Bitcoin in Kenya and local trading volume.

Mexico is an economy that relies on cash, with most Mexicans still using paper Mexican pesos. A 2018 PYMNTS survey estimated that 90% of transactions conducted by Mexican consumers were made in cash instead of digital payments or credit cards. This trend did not reverse with the COVID-19 pandemic—in fact, the share of cash on hand in the Mexican economy continues to grow.[175] Bitcoin has made inroads into the country, with a Bitcoin Embassy and bar that accepts Lightning payments prominently installed in the center of Mexico City. However, this is more peer-to-peer bottom-up demand than top-down authorization, with the Bank of Mexico coming out against Bitcoin after Mexican billionaire Ricardo Salinas Pleigo endorsed it on social media. The central bank reminded banks in Mexico that the country's financial institutions "are not authorized to conduct or offer to the public transactions with virtual assets like Bitcoin."[176]

The Choice Nation-States Face

Nation-states face a choice—should they try to aggressively pursue their own central bank digital currency and implement their version of control similar to China, or should they embrace Bitcoin and open-source technologies and let their peoples and a global community of builders collaborate to transact value with each other?

Why would a nation-state choose Bitcoin over a more internationalized and digital yuan or the USD or another basket of foreign currencies? First, most nations will not be able to develop digital payment rails at the scale and speed of how Bitcoin moves. Many problems are solved using the Bitcoin stack because it has had a game theory-proven effect on protecting digital keys across a large amount of digital wealth. The huge amounts attributed to Satoshi's billions have not moved an inch. The stack of services for custody, sending funds, and interfacing with exchange infrastructure is second to none. Companies spawned immediately to solve payment processing, wallet, and node transfer issues with the Lightning Network. If a nation-state wants to build digital payment rails from scratch, it would save time and work with a global system that can integrate with its fiat system. Just like many nations have visas for digital nomads, a nation-state can attract Bitcoin hodlers, a globally mobile class of entrepreneurs, to come over and spend their funds and time in the country in question. Employing the Bitcoin brand and being one of the early movers of nation-states ensures interaction with entrepreneurial talent that might well outweigh what a nation-state can do on its own. El Salvador and Bitcoin Beach show what can happen as a tourism hotspot mixed with the benefits of attracting different players in the Bitcoin ecosystem.

Unlike the Chinese yuan or the US dollar, Bitcoin is a participatory system where stakeholders worldwide align. Instead of becoming dependent on a country's currency and focusing on its interests first, anybody can be part of a community of builders that often disagree with one another but are building the ecosystem together. Smaller nations can have a much bigger say at the table by being one of the first nation-state stakeholders in the system. Bitcoin has proven that even "elites" at the very top do not always get their way. In the Blocksize Wars, the exchanges and big businesses that sought to increase the blocksize with Bitcoin (and thus make it more centralized, albeit more scalable) could not win out against users and developers.[177]

The early nation-states to adopt Bitcoin will hold Bitcoin in government treasuries—Bitcoin is meant to be deflationary and has tended to increase in value with each halving cycle. Early nation-state adopters might be rewarded with many rewards, especially as fiat currencies degrade. Many governments have fallen because of inflation. Bitcoin allows the citizens within a nation-state to be defended against the volatility of inflation by providing them with an independent option. In times of crisis, the USD has been a hedge everybody demands. In Lebanon, for example, during extreme hunger and inflation, people turned to the USD as a hedge—but in the future, they might choose Bitcoin.

There are reasons nation-states should hesitate to adopt Bitcoin as well. In a nation-state's eyes, the ability to control currency choices is an essential one. In many ways, the country's money is where a nation-state draws its power from everything, from its ability to pay agents to enforce its will in physical space to how it funds goods and services for the population. Not having control of a domestic currency means being accountable to other countries for financial and monetary infrastructure—creating a dependency of countries on other countries. This root fear is why many of the more authoritarian nations we examined are positioned the way they are against the Internet and Bitcoin. Yet this split doesn't just exist between "free" and "authoritarian" countries. The default for most nation-states is to preserve their powers and monopoly of currency and law enforcement. Multilateral organizations like the IMF have made it clear what they think about nation-states adopting Bitcoin, with strong condemnation of El Salvador's move to establish a nation-state-based treasury and to allow the use of Bitcoin as legal tender. Instead, the IMF is ready to support countries willing to adopt central bank digital currencies like what happened in Nigeria.[178]

For two decades, Bitcoin has been through social media attacks, nation-state bans, and various virtual risks almost without missing a beat. The large amounts assigned to Satoshi, with many billions of fiat dollars attached, have still not moved, showing that the system's security remains robust throughout decades. Bitcoin has been through multiple halving cycles and has seen many trading cycles. Nevertheless, it has not seen five decades or so of track record, or like some currencies, centuries. However, the gap in age may be smaller than one would think: modern currency is primarily framed up by what happened after World War II—which is about two generations of people away. That gap will still matter for nation-states who want to put their money and value in the most proven space possible, and ideally for a government that can project physical force.

Nation-states tend to organize themselves into blocs. Adapting another country's currency or even buying large amounts of it in reserve can sometimes come with favors owed to the nation-states to which those currencies belong. For example, there are trade agreements and other measures in order to increase the rate of trade flow between different countries, or there are nations that are dependent upon others for their physical security as a nation-state: Taiwan with the United States, Burma with China, and increasingly, Ukraine with the Western bloc. A standard critique of Bitcoin is that it is a solution looking for a problem in a world of nation-state choices. Time and energy are spent on a network replicating many of the critical traits already provided for those permissions within a powerful enough nation-state such as the United States.

This argument ignores those who are permissionless currently: those who live, through no fault of their own, in a country that is weak or that has run afoul of the current financial world order or those who have been rejected and are subjected to the worst fate of all: the fate of being stateless, of being rustled into nothingness and ill-treatment by other states and treated as a refugee at best. It also ignores weakly-permissioned people who still need state credentials to sign up for the financial system and be ingested into credit systems. However, when we look at the core of the argument, there is a grain of truth. Satoshi built Bitcoin in a context where the monopoly of state violence and currency that stemmed from it revolved around nation-states. Bitcoin can not only interoperate between different states, but it (and a host of new technologies) may allow the nation-state to evolve.

What would an evolution of nation-states look like? Most nation-states around the world are fundamentally similar with minor variations at a technical economic level: this is especially the case since the People's Republic of China embraced "socialism with Chinese characteristics" and fought hard to be a part of large, multilateral trade and finance organizations such as the World Trade Organization and the International Monetary Fund. The nation-state that embraces Bitcoin as a legal tender can evolve differently.

First, an international technical payments standard brings apparent changes. Allowing people to transact with one another and facilitating state support for the exchange of satoshis means that a nation-state has decided to invest monetary credibility into a decentralizing system. The

United States dollar and dollarized economies writ large were a massive feature of the late 21st century. However, in embracing a networked technology with no central authority, a nation-state that embraces Bitcoin (even as an alternative) places faith in a hedge that has not been seen before and does not have a central banker propping it up.

Bitcoin's security culture is growing due to the inclusion of nation-states and bottom-up demand from many stakeholders. Instead of driving toward a state-centered version of cybersecurity where states frantically try to enforce their standards and data protections (for example, in the case of China, which has strict local-origin laws on cybersecurity products and maintains that sensitive data must reside within China's geospatial borders), states and their people embrace more individualized, open-sourced, and game theory-tested versions of digital security and value.

Significant rewards are being placed on attacking the Bitcoin network, including in ways that affect individual users, such as phishing and phone takeovers. Services that draw from an international client list and an international talent pool to counter these threats have emerged. Examples include CasaHODL, which forms a suite of products, services, and education on the cutting edge of potential attacks on digital value. Open-source projects and documentation exist around the world when it comes to Bitcoin privacy and security, such as Bitcoin Wiki. In this way, the security and privacy ecosystem of online tools grows, not through top-down fiat and imposition but through bottom-up education and training motivated by real-world consequences.

In time, this bottom-up advocacy and learning has consequences beyond the economic and technological lens.

Bitcoin advances a form of democracy that advocates open debate on issues framed in tight technical constraints. However, anybody can participate and learn in the system with a few prerequisites. Everybody can start a node or set up a miner if motivated enough. Even the most complex legal constraints (for example, China's ban on mining enforced by its provincial administrations) can falter when it comes to pieces of commodity hardware and the simple need for a small quantity of electricity and knowledge in order to get started and to work within the Bitcoin network.

The Bitcoin network prioritizes digital security and understanding digital privacy—your keys, your funds, and your secure way to store those keys. Bitcoin is optimized around allowing for the public streaming of data while trying to minimize the amount of personal data collected to be a part of the network—in many cases, only an IP address (which is malleable and can be easily discarded) is needed to access and support Bitcoin. This same tendency can inspire people to be more autonomous and to think through systems of technological control, whether financial or those involving communications and data. In an era where technology tends to be a centralizing force, countries that turn to Bitcoin can inspire their people to communicate and exchange value with one another without the imposition of state force.

Ultimately, Bitcoin can spark a discussion on whether or not modern nation-states are the end-all and be-all of all governance. Can people at a sufficient scale gather together and coordinate without needing state force and hierarchy to enforce the proceeds of cooperation? Can humanity benefit from less violence, more health, and better education systems without needing to grant states the monopoly of violence? There are multiple avenues to a world without this overwhelming consensus of nation-states. There is the possibility of sub-state entities splitting off: a famous example is Scotland and its attempts to leave the United Kingdom. This nation-state independence can be done either peacefully or non-peacefully—an example of a war-like situation is the statelets that have been carved out de facto from the Arab Spring, from the autonomous Kurdish-controlled regions of Syria to the warring parts of Yemen. Any sub-state entity that seeks such a split will confront an immediate problem: having used the currency of its parent state for so long, it will have to either try to build an entirely new, unproven currency, continue using the currency of a state it is likely to be on poor terms with—or it can embrace Bitcoin. There are also free cities that exist within the framework of federal states that are confronting this issue. The most established is Prospera, which works within a set of constitutional changes from Honduras that permit ZEDE zones that act as autonomous special free trade zones. Yet Prospera itself must still live with the rules of Honduras, which can be modified—and one pressing example of this is that anybody who lives in Prospera has to be admitted under Honduran immigration law. Finally, new physical real estate could be molded by claiming large parts of the ocean and space, though this is unlikely to happen in the next decade at scale (but may in the next century). Even the Arctic territories that are freed up due to climate change will be coveted and fought over by physical states due to their availability for new, critical trade routes, the potential for arable land, and the rich amount of natural resources and commodities that will be available for plunder.

Instead of forcing nation-states to embrace a currency from another nation-state, Bitcoin offers a backdoor for individuals within a country, and ultimately, countries themselves, to break from this framework. Money without the state means people can decide to live outside the state in a meaningful, scaled way—and encrypted communications can bolster stateless money through different methods, from email and document sharing to chat. When governments have advanced repressive laws, such as the National Security Law in Hong Kong, their "governed" people have often replied with surges of downloads of applications such as Signal (encrypted chat) and VPNs that allow people to hide their Internet traffic geographically.

In a dialogue that has been almost exclusively dominated by nation-states, perhaps new technologies will also create a new form of organization for political power as well as the great worldwide "game" of geopolitics. Nation-states may choose to opt out of the currency war between the United States dollar and the yuan by taking the alternative of making Bitcoin legal tender. It is also possible that Bitcoin and related technologies might change the nature of nation-states themselves to be more responsive and careful to leverage new powers all-seeing data systems will give them.

Conclusion: The Future of Bitcoin

Satoshi emerged from nowhere, and still, to this day, it is impossible to see their nationality. The legacy Satoshi gave the world through Bitcoin has been ridiculed, dismissed, bolstered, and championed. It is a romantic origin story, a mystery on par with Srinivasa Ramanujan's ability to derive fundamental mathematical truths from his humble background as a clerk in a sari shop. While a work of genius, Ramanujan's work in pure mathematics opened up new lanes in research but was not an engineering innovation that had direct, short-term consequences for the world. Satoshi, an individual we may never know, provided the basis for a monetary system that did not rely on government or indeed any fiat authority to organize and offered the world a new possibility for diffusing financial (and ultimately) political power and all of the powers that drive from those—including the power to start wars, to kill at scale, and to control people. Satoshi created Bitcoin in the only possible way: by disappearing and leaving very few traces of which camp they were in and who they were. Nation-states can be petty and controlling. They sign treaties with each other to enforce their treatment of other citizens but regard the stateless with neglect or utter violence. Bitcoin's emergence can escape that framework by offering a mystery founder with few explicit ties and has helped clear the lines between country, ideology, and nationhood that drive inventions while delivering an innovation semi-free from the national myths that storm and battle one another in the darks.

Thanks to its creation story, Bitcoin is one of the first inventions of its scale with the best chance to be borderless. The stakes could not be higher—and it is unclear what will win. What is clear is that the friction caused by Bitcoin's drive to decentralize and China's techno-nationalist rise will be a reigning theme of the 21st century—and perhaps beyond. That it may have some of its most significant impact half a world away from the cryptography communities clustered in the Western United States is a testament to the inevitable rise of cryptography and the borderless need to dilute the power of tyrants wherever they are.

Appendix

Bitcoin's Price History

2009-2010

Before 2011, there isn't much to speak about when it comes to Bitcoin's price activity. Bitcoin is relatively unknown except for a few niche communities. People on Bitcoin-related forums, most notably Bitcointalk (where Satoshi used to post and was the co-founder), talked with one another informally and started the first peer-to-peer interactions on Bitcoin, including trading. Mt. Gox, one of the first Bitcoin exchanges, would start in 2010—with early ideas that Bitcoin needed a marketplace to truly succeed. It was in 2011 that BTC China, the first Chinese Bitcoin exchange, opened as well, showing an international appetite for Bitcoin started relatively early, and that Chinese citizens were also interested in this new technology.

Satoshi has frequent posts on Bitcointalk, mostly technical in nature as they are debugging issues and getting feedback from early users of Bitcoin. Their comments on the geopolitics of Bitcoin are strictly focused on keeping the young project alive: for example, writing about Wikileaks, he says that he "made the appeal to Wikileaks not to try to use Bitcoin," since Bitcoin was still early in its infancy. The "heat" of getting Bitcoin directly involved in a political fight might just destroy Bitcoin at that stage.

On August 15th, 2010, Satoshi also speculated about where the power generation will come from that will support Bitcoin's mining infrastructure. They openly think that mining will gravitate toward where power is free or discounted: perhaps not aware of how their open-source project will intersect with stranded power sources that needed to be liberated from top-down planning from hydroelectricity plants in China, but in general, thinking in terms of the system of incentives that will lead to this reality.

2011

In October of 2011, Litecoin came about as the first "altcoin"—beginning a debate between those who are portrayed as Bitcoin "maximalists" and the proponents of many different chains together. Litecoin's founder, Charlie Lee, is the brother of Bobby Lee, who founded one of the first Bitcoin exchanges in the world in China. Litecoin is the first altcoin with a significant effect on Bitcoin's price level as well, with a lower level of price for Bitcoin after its release.

Bitcoin mining was simple and could be done on a laptop. You could get tens of thousands of Bitcoin without much effort. Only during 2011 did the price gain parity with one US dollar, and then in a few months, it saw a price increase of around 30x—creating an initial spark for sophisticated price action. However, price history around this time is still murky as there aren't many public indexes of Bitcoin prices.

2012–2013

2012 was a pretty steady year for Bitcoin, with more developing interest around the world, but relatively stable price growth. Toward the end of 2013, there began an explosive price action. Bitcoin started to be worth $1,000 USD for one Bitcoin, a critical threshold. This represented thousands-times growth over the value of Bitcoin in a short period of time, meaning it went from a value of a few cents (and trading 10,000 BTC to a couple of pizzas) to having one Bitcoin represent significant amounts of fiat wealth. In June 2013, Mt. Gox, the largest Bitcoin exchange at the time, stopped processing US withdrawals, presaging its collapse. Baidu was early in terms of Chinese tech giants for accepting Bitcoin for different web security services. It was early enough in Bitcoin's history to see its potential, but not early enough for the Chinese party-state to really weigh in one way or another—until late in 2013 when the People's Bank of China prohibited financial institutions from dealing with Bitcoin, a warning shot across the bow on an emerging movement.

Bitcoin reacted by plunging in price, one of the first instances of macroeconomic instability and political censorship leading to a dent in the growing Bitcoin movement. 2013 also saw the founding of Bitmain, a company focused on providing mining hardware for Bitcoin. This was the beginning of converting Bitcoin from a hobbyist project to a viable economic force. Not only would there be dedicated hardware chips built specifically for Bitcoin, but Bitmain would also own some of the largest mining pools in the world—using software to assemble the economic rewards needed to dedicate mining supply to increasing sophistication.

Most of that action will be driven by Chinese entrepreneurs, leading to accusations that Bitcoin is controlled by China, as well as increasing amounts of state repression on Bitcoin at the same time. It will be Chinese entrepreneurs, many of them owning Internet cafes or other businesses, and some attracted to the idea of a money without government, that will innovate in the field. They'll defy top-down dictates from the provincial governments and eventually the State Council in order to both earn a profit—and for some, live according to their principles.

Ethereum was also described for the first time by founder Vitalik Buterin during late 2013 in an article in Bitcoin Magazine. Soon, Ethereum would become the largest altcoin to face Bitcoin, though it'll take a few years for this to take effect. For now Bitcoin is high in what is called Bitcoin dominance—the amount of market cap and trade value assigned to all cryptocurrencies. It's around 50% as of September 2023, but it used to be just Bitcoin and a bunch of small altcoins until Ethereum truly came along.

2013 would prove to be a pivotal year in Bitcoin's price history: it would mark the beginning of Bitcoin's long relationship with altcoins and exchanges, significant factors in the rise and fall of prices. It would also be the first year where Bitcoin would hop from hobbyist forums to more mainstream knowledge and public indexes and financial history.

Bitcoin Price December 31st, 2013: $767.74

2014

2014 was an incredible year of change in Bitcoin's price history, though the underlying trends that powered 2013 would be similar. 2013 showed short-term troubles at Mt.Gox, and its "hack" defined price action for the entire year. With the loss of around 750,000 BTC in user funds, the "hack" to this day is still in contention, with allegations that Mt. Gox's owners might have left with user funds. This caused Bitcoin's price to tumble.

Another trend that affected the change in Bitcoin price was the introduction and scaling of Bitmain in China. This presaged China becoming the big provider of Bitcoin supply, with most Bitcoin mining happening with mining pools and mining hardware that was developed by Chinese entrepreneurs. Midway through 2014, in April, the People's Bank of China would reach out and enact another layer of repression on Bitcoin, perhaps with an eye on what happened to Mt. Gox. By signaling to domestic banks and lenders that Bitcoin exchanges were now forbidden to access funds, the People's Republic of China hoped to use its top-down control of its bank reserves and financial system to crush the nascent technology early—despite the growing demand for Chinese entrepreneurs to get involved.

Toward the very end of the year, Bitcoin would see its first hard fork proposal, something that could threaten to split the chain into warring camps. It would turn into a full-scale war by next year, with all of the players in the Bitcoin ecosystem involved, including (most prominently) mining pools and exchange owners based out of China. It was a rough year for Bitcoin, which saw more than a halving when it came to price by the year.

Bitcoin Price January 1st, 2014: $772.53
Bitcoin Price December 31st, 2014: $313.33
Difference: -59.44% (bear market)

2015

2015 saw the block size wars, a major event in Bitcoin's history and a major factor in how it would be priced. A fundamental tension in Bitcoin has always been how many transactions you can process in a block. If you have to pay about the equivalent of a US dollar for every transaction that you do on Bitcoin, and if you need to wait for it to confirm on the chain, you could attempt to pay for coffee with Bitcoin and it would be both expensive and take more than thirty minutes.

Nowadays, that's often solved through the use of what are called Layer 2 solutions that help scale Bitcoin to the realm of using it for day-to-day transactions. However, back in 2015, this technology didn't exist. In 2015, a bitter war about Bitcoin's nature broke out, centered on block size.

Back when Satoshi still led the development of Bitcoin, he had imposed a 1MB block size limit: this meant that Bitcoin could only process about three to seven transactions a second. There were two factions: those who wanted the block size to be larger and to get the consensus of the network through a hard fork which would have forced changes on everybody with a Bitcoin node, and those who wanted to maintain the block size around the same size. Many Bitcoin mining pools and exchanges, some based in China, were big proponents of bigger blocks. However, Bitcoin Core developers tended toward keeping block size relatively flat or small.

Samson Mow, a representative of the "small block" faction, talked about how Bitmain's co-CEO, Jihan Wu, got personally involved, with a rallying cry around "firing the developers." Bitmain was once one of the largest, most dominant forces in Bitcoin, with a market cap projected around $40-50B just by itself. It was both a Bitcoin mining hardware provider as well as one of the largest mining pools in the Bitcoin ecosystem with Antpool. It was a Chinese company built by Chinese entrepreneurs that were interested in Bitcoin. Yet not only did it have to face scrutiny from the Chinese party-state, it also was divided by the Blocksize Wars within Bitcoin itself. Eventually, this would lead to Jihan Wu being ousted by his co-founder over the direction where he took Bitmain, putting Bitmain directly into the block size wars as a strong proponent of Bitcoin Cash and other forks that would help with Bitcoin's "scale."

What happened throughout was best summed up by Jonathan Bier's book "The Blocksize War: The Battle Over Who Controls Bitcoin's Protocol Rules." Roger Ver and others who owned Bitcoin.com took the side of Bitcoin Cash and increasing the block size. Most exchanges and professional Bitcoin businesses also went with Bitcoin Cash. It was the community and the maintainers of Bitcoin's code that resisted and warned against the effect of turning Bitcoin into another project focused on profit rather than principle. The community ended up winning out, and the implications of that marked it as a cornerstone moment of Bitcoin's history. At the end of the year, Bitcoin would move to be stronger in price than it was when it started the year.

> *Bitcoin Price January 1st, 2015: $314.35*
> *Bitcoin Price December 31st, 2015: $434.43*
> *Difference: 38.19% (slight bull market)*

2016

2016 would mark the second Bitcoin halving, and probably the first one that would involve Bitcoin at scale, given the amount of mining pools involved in securing the Bitcoin network by this point. In 2012, the first Bitcoin halving happened, but it would have nowhere near the effect it would have now. The halving is Bitcoin's price supply mechanism. There is a finite amount of Bitcoins that will ever be issued: the number is 21 million. To get there, the amount of Bitcoin a miner gets when they find a block, called the "block reward" halves about every 4 years. This was the first time a halving happened with Chinese entrepreneurs and hardware builders prominently involved. On block number 420,000, the miner who managed to unlock the block reward was the first to receive only 12.5 BTC instead of the block reward of 25 BTC right before it. The immediate effect is that the computing and hash rate dedicated to protecting Bitcoin goes down, as the reward for doing so declines.

Bitcoin would be poised for explosive growth next year—but 2016 would see the beginnings of that price movement, as Bitcoin neared the $1,000 mark by the end of the year, having more than doubled in price during the year.

Bitcoin Price January 1st, 2016: $434.33
Bitcoin Price December 31st, 2016: $998.05
Difference: 129.79% (bull market)

2017

2017 was the year where altcoin competition really took over. This was because Ethereum's first major use case at scale came to the fore in what were known as ICOs, or initial coin offerings. Ethereum allowed for the infrastructure to create tokens and altcoins at will without being that technical. This then led to an array of altcoins, which basically operated as a funding mechanism.

This year led to cryptocurrency market cap going up, but Bitcoin's dominance starting to fade, as exchanges and retail users were attracted to the yield of new tokens. Many of the people who missed Bitcoin's initial growth were now attracted to the idea of getting similar gains with Ethereum, or even riskier altcoins that would emerge. Bitcoiners could sit back and enjoy more than 12x return on their holdings if they held from the start to the end of 2017.

Bitcoin Price January 1st, 2017: $1,019.20
Bitcoin Price December 31st, 2017: $14,093.61
Difference: 1,282% (extreme bull market)

2018

After a year of rolling highs driven by altcoin action, 2018 was part of the first retrenchment cycle after explosive growth. January 2018 also had the first rumble of the Chinese party-state's desire to shut down mining operations. While governments in the West are now focused on making the same argument about environmental and energy waste, the Chinese party-state was acting rapidly.

By the end of 2018, Bitcoin fell to around $3,000 USD in value, marking a sharp drop from its 2017 peak. This came about as the "altcoin" fantasy had a quick surge and then drop, taking Bitcoin value with it. Since altcoins like Ripple could be issued at will by their creators and sold in whatever quantity needed, and since some of them could be "pre-mined" (i.e., held at will by any number of stakeholders), there became a rush to profit which not only duped retail investors but also gave governments, which were struggling with an approach toward Bitcoin, a promising avenue to advance anti-Bitcoin regulations: investor protection.

Bitcoin had now become associated with cryptocurrencies. Retail customers often had to buy Bitcoin or a stablecoin in order to trade in these new altcoins. The same exchanges that grew so powerful through offering customers the new option to trade in Bitcoin were increasingly putting their brand behind new altcoins, knowing that they could reap some of the investor interest for these altcoins into exchange fees.

2018 would be full of bearish sentiment, though those that maintained that Bitcoin should hold itself pure from altcoins had a moment of "I told you so." The altcoin vs. Bitcoin split would truly begin this year in the midst of one of Bitcoin's largest bear markets—with its value less than a third of what it was when the year started.

Bitcoin Price January 1st, 2018: $13,657.20
Bitcoin Price December 31st, 2018: $3,742.70
Difference: -172.59% (bear market)

2019

2019 was a year of recovery. There was beginning to be greater-level institutional support of Bitcoin, from public companies considering adding it to their treasury, to funds looking to get approved for a Bitcoin ETF.

With news of institutional support for Bitcoin, there was some recovery of Bitcoin's price levels toward the levels seen before January 2018, though still a bit off from the feverish pace set during the 2017 altcoin boom. Toward the latter half of 2019, the COVID-19 pandemic was set to start—creating immediate short-term movements in Bitcoin. COVID-19 would crash markets as equity markets tried to understand what the world would be like in the next few years. By now Bitcoin had broken out of its niche beginnings into a more sophisticated force. By 2019, institutional forces and more speculation led to Bitcoin's correlation with stock markets. As COVID-19 struck, the first thing that happened was a plunge in all "risky" assets, with Bitcoin's global infrastructure and 24/7 trading markets taking some of the brunt of this effect. However, as more people were exposed to digital censorship, failures with the traditional banking system, and more and more exposure to online e-commerce and activity, Bitcoin would be able to bounce back.

Bitcoin Price January 1st, 2019: $3,794.26
Bitcoin Price December 31st, 2019: $7,195.15
Difference: 89.6% (bull market)

2020

During the early stages of COVID-19, since Bitcoin was correlated with other assets and had a speculative element to it, the price crashed early. On March 17th, it fell to a low of nearly $4,000. This was a price level that hadn't been seen since the depths of the bear market in 2018, and marked a sharp difference from the run up to the 2017 ICO mania, which saw Bitcoin reach a high of nearly $15,000.

However, this year would mark the third halving of Bitcoin, with many more eyes and sophisticated mining equipment on the chain now. This would help with the price recovery somewhat, as Bitcoin supply would go down from here on out without major consequences for miners—a bullish symbol for the network's progress. In China, the Bitcoin halving helped ignite conversations in WeChat groups and other social media among those following the event. Miners were optimistic that they would continue to be provided reasonably cheap hydroelectric power and that there wouldn't be any mass state repression of Bitcoin mining yet. Yet trends were continuing to emerge that would help pave the way for further Bitcoin price action. The mining pools that dominated and aggregated Bitcoin mining hash rate around the world were now increasingly controlled not by hardware providers but exchanges.

For example, Binance would launch a mining pool in 2020 that within a month would become one of the top ten mining pools in the world. This further consolidated the power of exchanges in a shifting Bitcoin mining ecosystem, and allowed them to tap into Bitcoin being mined directly, as well as position themselves to offer liquidity services for Bitcoin miners.

China's party-state would also recognize "blockchain" jobs as a legitimate career path, continuing a long path of trying to paint cryptocurrency and Bitcoin as rogue, wasteful investment games, while looking to leverage "blockchain" as a frontier technology. It would portend a year of Chinese state policy designed to try to flesh out the difference and try to "crush" Bitcoin for Chinese citizens.

Bitcoin Price January 1st, 2020: $47,686.81
Bitcoin Price December 31st, 2020: $16,547.50
Difference: -65.29%

2021

It was in 2021 that the Chinese party-state tried to make its most crushing blow on Bitcoin yet, coordinated in a way that made it clear that Bitcoin had gone from a simple regulatory concern to a real threat to the Chinese party-state. Large cryptocurrency communities and exchanges would announce that they were shutting down their operations in mainland China. In May 2021, the State Council would finally call for a determined end to Bitcoin mining, and the provinces that had profited from this economic activity got the message and moved to shut down Bitcoin mining operations in their purview. For example, the Sichuan provincial government that had long been seen as lenient to Bitcoin miners, would tell 26 companies to immediately "clean up and terminate their mining operations."

This would lead to an inter-day drop in Bitcoin's price of more than 10%. Sichuan, home of the stranded hydroelectricity plants of years of top-down planning, had previously benefited from the taxes and jobs created through Bitcoin mining. Even when the central government had stated its intention to shut down Bitcoin mining at some time, this activity persisted. But now that the State Council had made its views clear, provincial governments could not stay on the fence anymore. Mining pools, many of them spinoffs from Chinese mining companies, would now make the decision not to ship their products to mainland China. Antpool, which spun off from Bitmain, was one of these groups. They also sought to block IP addresses from the mainland as well in order to demonstrate to the Chinese party-state that they were not trying to actively defy these new regulations.

Yet by the end of the year, Bitcoin's price would increase over where it started. 2021 showed that the Chinese party-state was serious about trying to ban Bitcoin—and how Bitcoin could bounce back from such an attack.

Bitcoin Price January 1st, 2021: $29,374.15
Bitcoin Price December 31st, 2021: $46,306.45
Difference: 57.64% (bull market)

2022

Since early 2022, macroeconomics and exchange failures have taken over Bitcoin's price history. Bitcoin lived throughout most of its history in an era of easy money. After the Great Recession, central banks around the world decided to run a radical experiment in monetary policy. Spooked by the freefall in stock markets and the freezing of credit that threatened the general economy, central banks set their policy interest rates close to zero and pursued an unconventional monetary policy that increased the monetary supply beyond levels that hadn't been seen before in world history. The only exception among this in global policy circles among the major economic powers was largely China. The People's Bank of China kept a fairly moderate monetary stance. Chinese policymakers and bankers openly slammed the West and claimed that they were protecting the value of money Chinese citizens had worked so hard to acquire.

Yet in 2022, these situations would invert. Central banks in the West were spooked by very high inflation readings. They started raising rates rapidly: from a decade of near-zero interest-rate policy to a time where the ECB was offering negative interest-rate policy, inflation caused Western central banks to tighten the reins. On the other hand, with a slowing real estate market, unfavorable demographics (caused by top-down one-child planning), and still trying to maintain a strict COVID-19 lockdown, the Chinese party-state found itself having to ease monetary concerns while the rest of the world was tightening.

During late November 2022, the FTX exchange (with roots in Hong Kong) would come undone, with another period of Bitcoin price instability about to correlated with an exchange failing again. The price action that comes with a significant exchange failing or not would drag down the price of Bitcoin even if a Bitcoiner didn't hold it on an exchange. By the end of 2022, Bitcoin's price would decline by about 65%, officially putting Bitcoin into bear market territory.

Bitcoin Price January 1st, 2022: $47,686.81
Bitcoin Price December 31st, 2022: $16,547.50
Difference: -165.29% (bear market)

2023

2023 was early on a time of relative price stability for Bitcoin, which has now cleared a certain price threshold: higher than the 2017 bull market, but less than the COVID price surge. Price action has gone up as ETFs involving Bitcoin have spawned. A big concern on the theme of exchanges is what will happen if the next shoe drops: for example, if Binance can no longer support itself, or if Tether deviates from its peg. There's also the possibility of more states taking action against Bitcoin: specifically, bans on Bitcoin mining and anti-crypto bills might start passing in Western countries. It's also likely that the SEC will continue to go after altcoin projects—with prosecutions on a civil level, and coordinating with the Department of Justice for criminal charges, to those the SEC deems to have done an "unregistered securities offering." In the long term, this will be bullish for Bitcoin, since the altcoins are a form of competition that drains away focus on the security of the Bitcoin network. Yet in the short term, many investors are going to get wrapped up in the correlation between altcoins and Bitcoin into a "cryptocurrency" package.

The flipside is also present in other facets. The next halving is in a year from now. In the grand scheme of things, Bitcoin now is worth half of a large technology company (Tesla or Apple). For a technology product, this might be a crowning feat. For a digital asset network that more and more people may store value in, this represents a massive opportunity.

Bitcoin Price January 1st, 2023: $16,625.08
Bitcoin Price December 31st, 2023: $42,265.19
Difference: 54.22% (bull market)

2024 and onwards

It can be hard to predict Bitcoin's price given that it's such a dynamic system—one where peer-to-peer demand takes hold. What has happened so far in 2024 has shown (if one reads the signs carefully enough) some trends for Bitcoin's price trends going forward.

First is the incredible price action as Bitcoin has cleared its previous all-time high, largely due to the approval of spot Bitcoin ETFs in the United States. These funds draw incredible inflows and are competing with one another to buy up whatever Bitcoin is left to trade from the people willing to sell rather than to hold. It's clear that the demand from ETFs and the inflows and outflows from them will play a large role in Bitcoin's price for the foreseeable future.

Second is the incredible growth of Layer 2 solutions, and proposals to make Bitcoin absorb more of Ethereum's capabilities on Layer 1. Technical improvements like OP_CAT and BitVM are aimed to make Layer 1 more versatile. It remains to be seen if replicating the ICO boom and NFT rush on Bitcoin will ultimately help the chain or hurt it, and there are strong advocates for both sides. Transaction fees for Layer 1 look set to increase in the short term as the "space" in Bitcoin is being filled with non-financial data—perhaps something that might solve a world without block mining rewards for miners, but also perhaps, in the words of some, "spam."

Third is the first halving to take place with a significant amount of Bitcoin mining shifted out of China—the first time this has happened in Bitcoin's history. Many mining companies now trade as public shares on American stock indexes, and are importing machines from China in order to install them at American sites. This is a sea change from much of Bitcoin's early history, and it remains to be seen how mining companies will react to having their mining rewards cut in half.

Finally, it's clear that the same factors that have always affected Bitcoin might be lurking again and that the system is incredibly volatile when it comes to simple demand and supply. There could be major exchanges or services that fail, or a government revealed to be buying Bitcoin en masse. Perhaps the most nuanced note we can end on is that plenty has happened in Bitcoin's price history and plenty more will happen: it helps to be intellectually humble and to readjust one's priors constantly when it comes to a dynamic peer-to-peer network like Bitcoin.

Endnotes

1   Julian Gewirtz, "The LittleKnown Story of Milton Friedman in China," Cato Institute Policy Report, September/October 2017, https://www.cato.org/policy-report/september/october-2017/little-known-story-milton-friedman-china#.

2   Chen Yulu, *Chinese Currency and the Global Economy* (Columbus, OH: McGraw Hill, 2014), 2.

3   Yulu, *Chinese Currency*, 6.

4   Helen Wang, "The Fabric of Banknotes – Textiles in and on Paper Money," in *Textile and Clothing along the Silk Roads*, eds. Feng Zhao and Marie Louise Nosch (Paris: UNESCO & China National Silk Museum, 2022), 335–46.

5   Jeffery Wasserstrom, *China in the 21st Century* (Oxford: Oxford University Press, 2013), 53.

6   Yulu, *Chinese Currency*, 20–21.

7   Madeleine Thien, "After the Cultural Revolution: What Western Classical Music Means in China," *The Guardian*, July 8, 2016, https://www.theguardian.com/music/2016/jul/08/after-the-cultural-revolution-what-western-classical-music-means-in-china.

8   Juan Du, *The Shenzhen Experiment: The Story of China's Instant City* (Cambridge: Harvard University Press, 2020).

9   "Panic Buying Clears Shelves in Chinese City; Inflation Spurs Record Bank Run," *Los Angeles Times*, August 16, 1988, https://www.latimes.com/archives/la-xpm-1988-08 -16-mn-711-story.html.

10   Li Yunqi, "China's Inflation: Causes, Effects, and Solutions," *Asian Survey* 29, no. 7 (July 1989): 655–668, https://doi.org /10.2307/2644672.

11   Interestingly, while the rush might have been to US dollars in the past, today it can be to Bitcoin.

12   W. L. Chong, "Price Reform in China: the Heated Summer 1988 Debates," *China Information* 3, no. 2 (1988): 1–11, https://doi.org/10.1177/0920203X8800300201.

13   Howard W. Sanderson and Michael Forsythe, *China's Superbank: Debt, Oil and Influence - How China Development Bank is Rewriting the Rules of Finance* (New York: Wiley, 2013), 51.

14   Sanderson and Forsythe, *China's Superbank*, 43.

15   Tommy Koh, "Deng Xiaoping and Singapore," Tembusu College, National University of Singapore, accessed January 28, 2024, https://tembusu.nus.edu.sg/news/2018/deng -xiaoping-and-singapore.

16   Colin Harper, "PayPal Co-Founder, Bitcoin Investor Thiel Says Bitcoin Could Be Chinese 'Weapon'," CoinDesk.com, last modified September 14, 2021, https://www.coindesk .com/markets/2021/04/07/paypal-co-founder-Bitcoin -investor-thiel-says-Bitcoin-could-be-chinese-weapon/.

17   Georgina Lee, "Bitmain, Canaan and Ebang IPO Plans Snared by Trump's Tariffs on Chinese Cryptocurrency Mining Gear," *South China Morning Post*, October 16, 2018, https://www.scmp.com/business/china-business /article/2168679/they-were-minting-money-making -cryptocurrency-mining-gear.

18   Eunice Rosenfeld, "Major Chinese Bitcoin Conference Flees to Hong Kong as Government Cracks Down on

Cryptocurrencies," *CNBC,* September 18, 2017, https://www
.cnbc.com/2017/09/18/cryptocurrencies-major-Bitcoin
-conference-flees-as-china-cracks-down.html.

19 "Beijing Bitcoin Meetup," *Meetup,* accessed January 31,
2024, https://www.meetup.com/beijingBitcoinmeetup
/?_cookie-check=cPZLieTCBTOikaNS.

20 "Blockchain Conferences in China 2024/2025/2026,"
Conference Index, accessed February 1, 2024, https://
conferenceindex.org/conferences/blockchain/china.

21 Bitmain, "2023 World Digital Mining Summit 2023,"
Bitmain, accessed January 31, 2024, https://www.bitmain
.com/wdmsGlobal/Hongkong?trk=public_post_comment
-text.

22 Matthew Wallerstein, "Who Develops and Funding
Bitcoin (BTC)?" *CoinsPaid Media,* October 10, 2023, https://
coinspaidmedia.com/Bitcoin/who-develops-and-funds
-Bitcoin-a-list-of-developers-and-related-organizations/.

23 Anna Zmudzinski, "15 Arrested in China for Allegedly
Bribing Internet Cafe to Mine Crypto," *Cointelegraph,*
September 4, 2019, https://cointelegraph.com/news/15
-arrested-in-china-for-allegedly-bribing-internet-cafe-to
-mine-crypto.

24 "比特币," 百度百科, accessed January 31, 2024, https://baike
.baidu.com/item/%E6%AF%94%E7%89%B9%E5%B8%81/.

25 "Repository Search 比特币," *Github,* accessed January 31,
2024, https://github.com/search?q=%
E6%AF%94%E7%89%B9%E5%B8%81/.

26 Zhengxu Song, "Global Chinese Diaspora," in *The Palgrave
Handbook of Ethnicity*, ed. S. Ratuva (Singapore: Palgrave
Macmillan, 2019), https://doi.org/10.1007/978-981-13-2898-
5_82.

27 "Bitcoin/CONTRIBUTING.md at master · Bitcoin/Bitcoin,"
GitHub, accessed January 31, 2024, https://github.com
/Bitcoin/Bitcoin/blob/master/CONTRIBUTING.md.

28 Raffaele Feng, "Desperate Chinese Investors Are Pouring Into the U.S., Japan," *The Wall Street Journal*, January 25, 2024, https://www.wsj.com/finance/stocks/chinese-investors-are-pouring-into-the-u-s-japan-386be98e.

29 Elaine Yu, "Laundromats and VPNs: How China's Crypto Traders Are Evading the Rules," *Wall Street Journal*, January 18, 2024, https://www.wsj.com/world/china/laundromats-and-vpns-how-chinas-crypto-traders-are-evading-the-rules-8511ebe8.

30 Xuefei Liang, *Bitcoin and Beyond: The Secret Wealth Protection Strategies of China's Elite High Net Worth Individuals*, Amazon, https://www.amazon.ca/Bitcoin-Beyond-Protection-Strategies-Individuals-ebook/dp/.

31 Daniel Wan, "Cryptocurrency in China: Over the Counter, Under the Table," *CoinDesk*, August 5, 2019, https://www.coindesk.com/tech/2019/08/05/cryptocurrency-in-china-over-the-counter-under-the-table/.

32 "揭秘比特币场外地下交易：微信群主日撮合30万，月赚9万元," 投资界, October 31, 2017, https://m.pedaily.cn/news/422014.

33 Chainalysis Team, "Eastern Asia Cryptocurrency Adoption 2023," *Chainalysis*, October 2, 2023, https://www.chainalysis.com/blog/eastern-asia-cryptocurrency-adoption/.

34 Chainalysis Team, "APAC Report Preview: Why Tether Dominates in China," *Chainalysis*, October 15, 2019, https://www.chainalysis.com/blog/tether-china-apac-report-preview/.

35 "Tether Appoints Paolo Ardoino as CEO | Oct 13 2023," *Tether*, accessed March 31, 2024, https://tether.to/en/tether-appoints-paolo-ardoino-as-ceo/.

36 Tomislav Franjkovic, "China Dashes Crypto Hopes Again, Hailing Zhao Dong's Prison Sentence," *CCN.com*, December 28, 2023, https://www.ccn.com/news/china-crypto-zhao-dongs-prison-sentence/.

37 Zoltan Faux et al., "Crypto Mystery: Where's the $69 Billion Backing the Stablecoin Tether?" *Bloomberg.com*, October 7, 2021, https://www.bloomberg.com/news/features /2021-10-07/crypto-mystery-where-s-the-69-billion-backing -the-stablecoin-tether/.

38 "Understanding Tether's Peg and Reserves | May 23 2022," *Tether*, accessed January 31, 2024, https://tether.to/en /understanding-tethers-peg-and-reserves/.

39 David Jeans and Steven Emerson, "Billions Of Tether's Reserves Were Stored At Cantor Fitzgerald, Capital Union And Ansbacher," *Forbes*, February 10, 2023, https://www .forbes.com/sites/davidjeans/2023/02/10/tether-reserves -cantor-capital-union-ansbacher/?sh=251899de4928.

40 "Tether to Further Strengthen Reserves Through Purchase of Bitcoin with Realized Net Operating Profits," *Tether*, May 17, 2023, https://tether.to/en/tether-to-further-strengthen -reserves-through-purchase-of-Bitcoin-with-realized-net -operating-profits/.

41 Helen Partz, "China calls for crackdown on Tether stablecoin over illegal forex trading," *Cointelegraph*, December 29, 2023, https://cointelegraph.com/news/china -tether-crackdown-illegal-forex.

42 Federal Reserve Board, "Central Bank Digital Currency (CBDC)," *Federal Reserve Board*, accessed February 1, 2024, https://www.federalreserve.gov/central-bank-digital -currency.htm.

43 IMF, "Behind the Scenes of Central Bank Digital Currency: Emerging Trends, Insights, and Policy Lessons," *International Monetary Fund*, February 9, 2022, https://www .imf.org/en/Publications/fintech-notes/Issues/2022/02/07 /Behind-the-Scenes-of-Central-Bank-Digital-Currency -512174.

44 Evan Osnos, *Age of Ambition: Chasing Fortune, Truth, and Faith in the New China* (Farrar, Straus and Giroux, 2015).

45 Bailey Hu, "China's list of richest individuals gets 14 new blockchain entrepreneurs," *TechNode*, October 10, 2018, https://technode.com/2018/10/10/hurun-china-rich-list-blockchain/.

46 "ASICMINER: Entering the Future of ASIC Mining by Inventing It," *BitcoinTalk*, https://Bitcointalk.org/index.php?topic=99497.26780.

47 "ASICs and entrepreneurs: The founding of China's first mining pool," *F2pool.io*, https://f2pool.io/mining/insights/20201209-founding-chinas-first-mining-pool/.

48 It is worth noting that the first mining pools did not start in China: in 2010 a Czech entrepreneur created Slushpool, the oldest surviving Bitcoin mining pool. See "Our Mining Pool Story," *Braiins Pool*, https://braiins.com/pool/story?utm_source=BraiinsPool.

49 Daniel Pan, "Our Mining Pool Story," *Coindesk*, January 26, 2021, https://www.coindesk.com/business/2021/01/26/bitmain-co-founder-exits-resolving-years-long-power-struggle-as-mining-firm-preps-ipo/.

50 Natasha Lomas, "After Silk Road Closure, And With Baidu's Blessing, Bitcoin Breaks $200 Again," *TechCrunch*, October 22, 2013, https://techcrunch.com/2013/10/22/Bitcoin-breaks-200-again/.

51 Joon Ian Wong, "Huobi Sends $400k to Wrong User Accounts," *Coindesk*, November 9, 2017, https://www.coindesk.com/markets/2014/09/25/huobi-sends-400k-to-wrong-user-accounts/.

52 "SEC Files 13 Charges Against Binance Entities and Founder Changpeng Zhao," U.S. Securities and Exchange Commission, October 1, 2023, https://www.sec.gov/news/press-release/2023-101.

53 St. Louis Fed, "M2 (M2SL) | FRED | St. Louis Fed," Federal Reserve Economic Data, accessed January 31, 2024, https://fred.stlouisfed.org/series/M2SL.

54 Alejandro Fernández et al., "Capital Control Measures: A New Dataset," *IMF Economic Review* 64, no. 3 (2016): 548–574, http://www.jstor.org/stable/45212119.

55 Joon Ian Wong, "BTCC's Bobby Lee: Chinese Capital Controls Not a Factor in Recent Bitcoin Price Rise," *Bitcoin Magazine*, June 24, 2016, https://Bitcoinmagazine.com/culture/btcc-s-bobby-lee-chinese-capital-controls-not-a-factor-in-recent-Bitcoin-price-rise-1466783170.

56 "Canadian Banks Help Chinese Flout Their Laws to Get Piece of 'Smurfing' Billions," *Financial Post*, accessed January 16, 2024, https://financialpost.com/investing/global-investor/canadian-banks-help-chinese-flout-their-laws-to-get-piece-of-smurfing-billions.

57 Sean Foley, Jonathan R. Karlsen, and Tālis J. Putniņš, "Sex, drugs, and Bitcoin: How much illegal activity is financed through cryptocurrencies?" January 16, 2024, https://papers.ssrn.com/sol3/papers.cfm?abstract_id=3956933.

58 Xiaoyang Yu and Xianguo Zhou, "Income inequality in today's China," *Proceedings of the National Academy of Sciences* 111, no. 19 (2014): 6928–6933, https://doi.org/10.1073/pnas.1403158111.

59 Unlike previous leaders, Xi Jinping has outlasted the ten-year term limit that Deng put in place to stop "another Mao."

60 David Folkenflik, "Bloomberg News Killed Investigation, Fired Reporter, Then Sought to Silence his Wife," *NPR*, April 14, 2020, https://www.npr.org/2020/04/14/828565428/bloomberg-news-killed-investigation-fired-reporter-then-sought-to-silence-his-wi.

61 Zhimin Li, Leslie Sheng Shen, and Calvin Zhang, "Local Effects of Global Capital Flows: A China Shock in the U.S. Housing Market," *The Review of Financial Studies* 37, no. 3 (2023): 761–801, https://doi.org/10.1093/rfs/hhad067.

62 Sebastian Rotella and Kirsten Berg, "Operation Fox Hunt: How China Exports Repression Using a Network of Spies Hidden in Plain Sight," *ProPublica*, October 26, 2023, https://www.propublica.org/article/operation-fox-hunt -how-china-exports-repression-using-a-network-of-spies -hidden-in-plain-sight.

63 Isabel Kaminski, "Chinese court rules Bitcoin mining harms the climate," *Climate Home News*, July 21, 2022, https://www.climatechangenews.com/2022/07/21/chinese -court-rules-Bitcoin-mining-harms-the-climate/.

64 Shuheng Jiang et al., "Policy assessments for the carbon emission flows and sustainability of Bitcoin blockchain operation in China," *Nature Communications* 12 (2021), https://doi.org/10.1038/s41467-021-22256-3.

65 This section draws from the Coindesk piece on the same topic but dives deeper, adds more events, and looks at more context for how its series of Bitcoin bans changed the Chinese state. See Alexander Sergeenkov, "China Crypto Bans: A Complete History," CoinDesk, September 29, 2021, https://www.coindesk.com/learn/china-crypto -bans-a-complete-history/.

66 "人民银行等五部委发布关于防范比特币风险的通知," 中国政府网, December 5, 2013, https://www.gov.cn/gzdt/2013-12/05 /content_2542751.htm.

67 Charles Riley Deng, "People's Bank of China Official Blogs His Skepticism About Bitcoin," *The Wall Street Journal*, March 31, 2014, https://www.wsj.com/articles/SB1000142405 27023041572045794733390236208608.

68 Charles Riley Deng and Lingling Wei, "China Central Bank Orders Firms to Close Bitcoin Trading Accounts in Two Weeks," *The Wall Street Journal*, April 1, 2014, https://www.wsj. com/articles/SB100014240527023041572045794752338795 06454.

69 BTCC, "BTCC on X: "4/ BTCChina Exchange and BTCChina Blockchain+ have enough funds to accommodate all

customer withdrawals, including CNY, BTC, LTC, BCC, & ETH,"" *X.com*, September 15, 2017, https://twitter.com/BTCC exchange/status/908647813491318785.

70 Zheping Huang, "China wants an 'orderly exit' from Bitcoin mining," Quartz, January 8, 2018, https://qz.com /1174091/china-wants-an-orderly-exit-from-Bitcoin-mining.

71 Weiyi Yujian, Hu Yue, and Kang Baili, "Blockchain News Accounts Booted From WeChat," *Caixin Global*, August 22, 2018, https://www.caixinglobal.com/2018-08-22/blockchain -news-accounts-booted-from-wechat-101317720.html.

72 Dandan Li, "潘功胜：坚决打击遏制虚拟货币交易、ICO融资-新闻," 上海证券报, August 23, 2018, https://news.cnstock .com/news,yw-201808-4262742.htm.

73 中国人民银行, "中国人民银行关于《中华人民共和国中国人民银行法（修订草案征求意见稿）》公开征求意见的通知_国务院部门文件," 中国政府网, October 23, 2020, https://www.gov.cn /zhengce/zhengceku/2020-10/24/content_5553847.htm.

74 "中国互联网金融协会、中国银行业协会、中国支付清算协会：防范虚拟货币交易炒作风险-新闻," 上海证券报, May 18, 2021, https://news.cnstock.com/news,bwkx-202105-4704916.htm.

75 Jamie Redman, "Sichuan's Blockchain Park: Chengdu Government Officials Welcome Bitcoin Miners," *Bitcoin. com News*, September 2, 2020, https://news.Bitcoin.com /sichuans-blockchain-park-chengdu-government-officials -welcome-Bitcoin-miners/.

76 Ying Shuang and Feng Zhou, "Poverty alleviation in Sichuan: Villagers begin moving into new homes," *CGTN*, April 28, 2020, https://news.cgtn.com/news/2020-04-28 /Poverty-alleviation-in-Sichuan-Villagers-begin-moving -into-new-homes-Q3mwl3tXDq/index.html.

77 Namcios, "Sichuan Shuts Down Bitcoin Miners," *Bitcoin Magazine*, June 18, 2021, https://Bitcoinmagazine.com /business/sichuan-shuts-down-Bitcoin-miners.

78 Alexander Asmakov, "After Bitcoin Mining, China Cracks

Down on Crypto Influencers on Weibo," *Decrypt*, June 7, 2021, https://decrypt.co/72920/after-Bitcoin-mining-china-cracks-down-crypto-influencers-weibo.

79 Rebecca Huang, "After China's Bitcoin Mining Ban, Bitcoin is Stronger Than Ever," *Forbes*, October 31, 2023, https://www.forbes.com/sites/digital-assets/2023/10/31/after-chinas-Bitcoin-mining-ban-Bitcoin-is-stronger-than-ever/?sh=693fdd732399.

80 Arjun Kharpal, "China looks to become blockchain world leader with Xi Jinping backing," *CNBC*, December 16, 2019, https://www.cnbc.com/2019/12/16/china-looks-to-become-blockchain-world-leader-with-xi-jinping-backing.html.

81 Electronic Information Department, Information Technology Development Department, Ministry of Industry and Information Technology, "大力发展新一代信息技术产业！"新时代工业和信息化发展"系列主题新闻发布会第九场实录来了," 中国工信产业网, September 20, 2022, https://www.cnii.com.cn/tx/202209/t20220920_415572.html.

82 Paul Morinville, "A Journey Through the Chinese Patent System," *IPWatchdog.com*, 2018, https://ipwatchdog.com/2018/10/07/journey-chinese-patent-system/id=102117/.

83 "Chinese Patent Data Project - SIPO - Chinese listed firms," *Google Sites*, accessed February 3, 2024, https://sites.google.com/site/sipopdb/cpdp-home/sipo-chinese-listed-firms.

84 Shihoko Goto and Graham Green, "Blockchain in China," Stimson Center, August 16, 2021, https://www.stimson.org/2021/blockchain-in-china/.

85 Omkar Godbole and David Pan, "Bitcoin Falls as Chinese Official Calls for Mining Crackdown," *CoinDesk*, May 21, 2021, https://www.coindesk.com/markets/2021/05/21/bitcoin-falls-as-china-calls-for-crackdown-on-crypto-mining-trading/.

86 Jeremy Goldkorn, "A Bitcoin mine in the mountains of

Sichuan," *The China Project*, December 6, 2016, https://thechinaproject.com/2016/12/06/eric-mu-Bitcoin-mine/.

87 "Elder Liu He remains China's economic guide, including on US strategy," *South China Morning Post*, June 23, 2023, https://finance.yahoo.com/news/elder-liu-remains-chinas-economic-093000502.html.

88 Hanif Maishera, "Coinmarketcap And Coingecko Ban Shows China Is Cracking Down Hard On Cryptocurrencies," *Yahoo Finance*, September 28, 2021, https://finance.yahoo.com/news/coinmarketcap-coingecko-ban-shows-china-112511027.html.

89 Zheping Yang, "Outlawing VPNs and More Protection of Personal Data: China Releases Draft Cyber Data Security Administrative Rules," *Protocol*, November 18, 2022, https://www.protocol.com/china/vpns-out-new-cyber-regulation.

90 Daisuke Wakabayashi, "Inside Apple's Compromises in China: A Times Investigation," *The New York Times*, June 17, 2021, https://www.nytimes.com/2021/05/17/technology/apple-china-censorship-data.html.

91 Aisha Malik, "Decentralized social networking app Damus to be removed from App Store, will appeal decision," *TechCrunch*, June 26, 2023, https://techcrunch.com/2023/06/26/decentralized-social-networking-app-damus-to-be-removed-from-app-store-will-appeal-decision/.

92 Zhaoyin Feng, "Why China's Bitcoin miners are moving to Texas," *BBC News*, September 3, 2021, https://www.bbc.com/news/world-us-canada-58414555.

93 "Chinese Court Rules Bitcoin Miner Sales Contract Invalid," *LexBlog*, accessed January 26, 2024, https://www.lexblog.com/2023/06/26/chinese-court-rules-Bitcoin-miner-sales-contract-invalid/.

94 King & Wood Mallesons, "Cryptocurrency is 'property' under Hong Kong law: Part 1 - what are the key

implications and what is the judicial position in Mainland China?," *Lexology*, May 8, 2023, https://www.lexology.com/library/detail.aspx?g=cde5d269-cef3-4bca-8011-aa2c32 194959.

95 "China Proposes Global Rules for Managing Sovereign Digital Currencies," *China Briefing*, April 4, 2021, https://www.china-briefing.com/news/china-proposes-global-rules-for-managing-sovereign-digital-currencies/.

96 Adrian Stephan, "Knowledge Base: Digital Currency Research Institute (数字货币研究所) of the People's Bank of China," March 8, 2022, https://digichina.stanford.edu/work/knowledge-base-digital-currency-research-institute-of-the-peoples-bank-of-china/.

97 Chun Han Wong, "China Is Now Sending Twitter Users to Prison for Posts Most Chinese Can't See," *The Wall Street Journal*, January 21, 2021, https://www.wsj.com/articles/china-is-now-sending-twitter-users-to-prison-for-posts-most-chinese-cant-see-11611932917.

98 Paul Mozur, "Zoom Blocks Activist in U.S. After China Objects to Tiananmen Vigil," *The New York Times*, June 17, 2020, https://www.nytimes.com/2020/06/11/technology/zoom-china-tiananmen-square.html.

99 Tom Blackwell, "Censored by a Chinese tech giant? Canadians using WeChat app say they're being blocked," *National Post*, December 4, 2019, https://nationalpost.com/news/censored-by-a-chinese-tech-giant-canadians-using-wechat-app-say-theyre-being-restricted.

100 Romina Turrin, "Why China's digital yuan will not kill off Alipay and WeChat Pay," *South China Morning Post*, February 15, 2022, https://www.scmp.com/comment/opinion/article/3166958/chinas-digital-yuan-not-death-knell-alipay-and-wechat-pay.

101 Kane Zhai and Julie Zhu, "Exclusive: China's central bank urges antitrust probe into Alipay, WeChat Pay – sources,"

Reuters, July 31, 2020, https://www.reuters.com/article/us
-alipay-wechat-pay-china-exclusive-idUSKCN24W0XD/.

102 Arjun Kharpal, "China's ICBC, the world's biggest bank,
hit by cyberattack that reportedly disrupted Treasury
markets," *CNBC*, November 10, 2023, https://www.cnbc
.com/2023/11/10/icbc-the-worlds-biggest-bank-hit-by
-ransomware-cyberattack.html

103 Lily Hay Newman, "Chinese Police Exposed 1B People's
Data in Unprecedented Leak," *WIRED*, July 9, 2022, https://
www.wired.com/story/chinese-police-exposed-1-billion
-peoples-data/.

104 Matt Burgess, "Ignore China's New Data Privacy Law at
Your Peril," *WIRED*, November 5, 2021, https://www.wired
.com/story/china-personal-data-law-pipl/.

105 Thomas B. Elston, "Future of the Digital yuan," *Foreign
Policy Research Institute*, June 2, 2023, https://www.fpri
.org/article/2023/06/china-is-doubling-down-on-its-digital
-currency/.

106 "深圳的数字货币"红包"试验谁最受益?," 新浪, *Finance Sina*,
October 29, 2020, https://finance.sina.com.cn/blockchain
/coin/2020-10-29/doc-iiznezxr8729207.shtml.

107 Sun Jing and Zhang Maohua, "Digital yuan continues
domestic march," *China Daily - Global Edition*, December
27, 2022, https://global.chinadaily.com.cn/a/202212/27
/WS63aa2668a31057c47eba6406.html.

108 Working Group on E-CNY Research and Development
of the People's Bank of China, "Progress of Research &
Development of E-CNY in China," People's Bank of China,
July 15, 2021, http://www.pbc.gov.cn/en/3688110/3688172
/4157443/4293696/2021071614584691871.pdf.

109 Mamat Nulimaimaiti, "What's the state of China's digital
yuan in 2023?," *South China Morning Post*, October 10, 2023,
https://www.scmp.com/economy/china-economy
/article/3237317/whats-state-chinas-digital-yuan-2023.

110 Amit Kumar, "A Report Card on China's Central Bank Digital Currency: the e-CNY," *Atlantic Council*, March 1, 2022, https://www.atlanticcouncil.org/blogs /econographics/a-report-card-on-chinas-central -bank-digital-currency-the-e-cny/.

111 Shi Jing, "Digital yuan continues domestic march," *China Daily - Global Edition*, December 27, 2022, https://global .chinadaily.com.cn/a/202212/27/WS63aa2668a31057c47eba 6406.html.

112 John Coghlan, "Former Chinese central banker says digital yuan 'usage has been low'," *Cointelegraph*, December 30, 2022, https://cointelegraph.com/news/former-chinese -central-banker-says-digital-yuan-usage-has-been-low.

113 "China Will Steadily Promote yuan Internationalisation in 2021, Central Bank Says," *Reuters*, November 9, 2017, https: //www.reuters.com/article/china-economy-yuan -internationlisation-idUSL1N2QK057/.

114 Serkan Arslanalp and Carleigh Simpson-Bell, "US dollar share of global foreign exchange reserves drops to 25-year low," International Monetary Fund, May 5, 2021, https://www.imf. org/en/Blogs/Articles/2021/05/05/blog-us-dollar-share-of- global-foreign-exchange-reserves-drops-to-25-year-low.

115 Andrea Nicita and Carlos Razo, "China: Rise of the trade titan," *UNCTAD*, April 27, 2021, https://unctad.org/news /china-rise-trade-titan.

116 Eyal Dahan and Ali El Yaakoubi, "China's Xi calls for oil trade in yuan at Gulf summit in Riyadh," *Reuters*, December 10, 2022, https://www.reuters.com/world /saudi-arabia-gathers-chinas-xi-with-arab-leaders-new -era-ties-2022-12-09/.

117 William Bianchi and Samantha Morland, "Argentina to pay for Chinese imports in yuan rather than dollars," *Reuters*, April 26, 2023, https://www.reuters.com/world /china/argentina-govt-pay-chinese-imports-yuan-rather -than-dollars-2023-04-26/.

118 "How MBridge cross border CBDC encourages foreign digital yuan use," *Ledger Insights*, November 1, 2022, https://www.ledgerinsights.com/mbridge-cbdc-encourages -digital-yuan/.

119 Working Group on E-CNY, "Progress of Research & Development."

120 Jamie McGeever, "China slips away from Treasuries but sticks with dollar bonds," *Reuters*, February 22, 2023, https://www.reuters.com/markets/asia/china-slips-away -treasuries-sticks-with-dollar-bonds-2023-02-22/.

121 Changchun Mu, "Balancing Privacy and Security: Theory and Practice of the E-CNY's Managed Anonymity," People's Bank of China, http://www.pbc.gov.cn/en/3935690/393575 9/4696666/2022110110364344083.pdf.

122 Lyric Maizland and James M. Lindsay, "Hong Kong's Freedoms: What China Promised and How It's Cracking Down," Council on Foreign Relations, February 3, 2024, https://www.cfr.org/backgrounder/hong-kong-freedoms -democracy-protests-china-crackdown.

123 Roger Huang, "Hong Kong Cryptocurrency Hub Gives Bitcoin Cash-Funded Water To Protestors," *Forbes*, August 19, 2019, https://www.forbes.com/sites/rogerhuang /2019/08/19/hong-kong-cryptocurrency-hub-gives-Bitcoin -cash-funded-water-to-protestors/.

124 "Statement on Security Token Offerings," Securities & Futures Commission of Hong Kong, March 28, 2019, https://www.sfc.hk/en/News-and-announcements/Policy -statements-and-announcements/Statement-on-Security -Token-Offerings.

125 "Hong Kong Bitcoin Regulation," The Bitcoin Association of Hong Kong, February 4, 2021, https://www.Bitcoin.org .hk/hong-kong-Bitcoin-regulation/.

126 "Pay with Bitcoin," The Bitcoin Association of Hong Kong, February 4, 2021, https://www.Bitcoin.org.hk/pay-with -Bitcoin/.

127 Gareth Lee, "Hong Kong's leading crypto retail operator says it ceases trading as FTX fallout roils sector," *Reuters*, November 18, 2022, https://www.reuters.com/technology/hong-kongs-leading-crypto-retail-operator-says-it-ceases-trading-ftx-fallout-2022-11-18/.

128 Lee, "Hong Kong's leading crypto."

129 Nelly Wang, "FTX Moves Headquarters From Hong Kong to Bahamas," *CoinDesk*, September 24, 2021, https://www.coindesk.com/business/2021/09/24/ftx-moves-headquarters-from-hong-kong-to-bahamas-report/.

130 Paul Riordan and Cannix Yau, "How FTX used Hong Kong cash-for-crypto shop to turbocharge growth," *Financial Times*, December 5, 2022, https://www.ft.com/content/68dbe10a-fa38-443a-9790-dc96f2d8979a/.

131 Harald Braun, "Bitcoin ETF (BTC) In-Kind Creations Likely in Hong Kong," *CoinDesk*, March 26, 2024, https://www.coindesk.com/business/2024/03/26/hong-kong-likely-to-allow-in-kind-creations-for-spot-bitcoin-etfs-bloomberg/.

132 Marvin Emem, "Crackdown on Crypto Conversion Shops Coming to Hong Kong, According to Regulators: Report," *The Daily Hodl*, February 28, 2024, https://dailyhodl.com/2024/02/28/crackdown-on-crypto-conversion-shops-coming-to-hong-kong-according-to-regulators-report/.

133 Yaxue Du, "A Social Media Profile of the Late Dr. Li Wenliang: From a Liberal-leaning Student, to a Party Adherent, to a Whistleblower Who Believes a Society Should Have More Than One Voice," *China Change*, February 26, 2020, https://chinachange.org/2020/02/26/a-social-media-profile-of-the-late-dr-li-wenliang-from-a-liberal-leaning-student-to-a-party-adherent-to-a-whistleblower-who-believes-a-society-should-have-more-than-one-voice/.

134 任 說 公, "不要让中国退回到朝鲜！——张展,"
Primal, March 28, 2024, https://primal.net/e/
note1kf4lmg2nk3q4eqc2zhf9g6e7peklvucr
0aekkhfcwtvvpah43zsn5undj.

135 Emily Feng, "China's authorities are quietly rounding up
people who protested against COVID rules," *NPR*, January
11, 2023, https://www.npr.org/2023/01/11/1148251868/china
-covid-lockdown-protests-arrests.

136 Douglas Vincent, "'One day everyone will use China's
digital currency'," *BBC*, September 24, 2020, https://www
.bbc.com/news/business-54261382.

137 Lily Cheng and Lynn White, "Elite Transformation and
Modern Change in Mainland China and Taiwan: Empirical
Data and the Theory of Technocracy," *The China Quarterly*
121 (1990): 1–35, http://www.jstor.org/stable/654061.

138 James Senior, "Opinion | 95 Percent of Representatives
Have a Degree. Look Where That's Got Us," *The New York
Times*, December 21, 2020, https://www.nytimes
.com/2020/12/21/opinion/politicians-college-degrees.html.

139 Cheng and White, "Elite Transformation."

140 His family background certainly helped him as well; his
father was Xi Zhongxun, whose Northwestern guerilla
base helped end Mao's Long March and who was part
of the first generation of Chinese Communist Party
leadership.

141 Philip Ping, "The Great Firewall of China: Background
Torfox," *Stanford Computer Science*, June 1, 2011, https://
cs.stanford.edu/people/eroberts/cs181/projects/2010-11
/FreedomOfInformationChina/the-great-firewall-of-china
-background/index.html.

142 Maggie Hu, "The Great Firewall: a technical perspective
Torfox," *Stanford Computer Science*, May 30, 2011, https://
cs.stanford.edu/people/eroberts/cs181/projects/2010-11
/FreedomOfInformationChina/great-firewall-technical
-perspective/index.html.

143 Lorand Laskai and Adam Segal, "The Encryption Debate in China: 2021 Update," Carnegie Endowment for International Peace, March 31, 2021, https://carnegie endowment.org/2021/03/31/encryption-debate-in-china -2021-update-pub-84218.

144 "China Enacts Encryption Law," Covington & Burling LLP, October 31, 2019, https://www.cov.com/-/media/files /corporate/publications/2019/10/china_enacts_encryption _law.pdf.

145 Evangelia Gkritsi, "China to Release National Blockchain Standard Next Year, Says Official: Report," *CoinDesk*, October 27, 2021, https://www.coindesk.com/policy /2021/10/28/china-to-release-national-blockchain-standard -next-year-says-official-report/.

146 Elmira Najmehchi, "Correcting the record on China's 'social credit system'," China Daily - Global Edition, November 29, 2019, https://global.chinadaily.com. cn/a/201911/29/WS5de0be2ea310cf3e3557af1a.html.

147 Jeremy Daum, "China through a glass, darkly," *China Law Translate*, December 24, 2017, https://www.chinalaw translate.com/en/china-social-credit-score/.

148 "Guangdong Provincial Social Credit Regulations," *China Law Translate*, March 26, 2021, https://www.china lawtranslate.com/en/guandong-provincial-social-credit/.

149 "Giving Credit 2: Carrots and Sticks," *China Law Translate*, December 15, 2017, https://www.chinalawtranslate.com/en /giving-credit-2-carrots-and-sticks/.

150 Lily Kuo, "China bans 23m from buying travel tickets as part of 'social credit' system," *The Guardian*, March 1, 2019, https://www.theguardian.com/world/2019/mar/01/china- bans-23m-discredited-citizens-from-buying-travel-tickets- social-credit-system/.

151 Ryan Martinez Mitchell, "Chinese Receptions of Carl Schmitt Since 1929," 8 *Pennsylvania State Journal of Law & International Affairs* 181 (2020), https://elibrary.law.psu.edu /jlia/vol8/iss1/8.

152 Robert Mitchell, "Schmitt in Beijing," *Critical Legal Thinking*, October 18, 2021, https://criticallegalthinking.com/2021/10/18/schmitt-in-beijing/.

153 "Carl Schmitt," *Stanford Encyclopedia of Philosophy*, last modified August 7, 2010, https://plato.stanford.edu/entries/schmitt/#SovDic.

154 "China's Algorithms of Repression: Reverse Engineering a Xinjiang Police Mass Surveillance App," *Human Rights Watch*, May 1, 2019, https://www.hrw.org/report/2019/05/01/chinas-algorithms-repression/reverse-engineering-xinjiang-police-mass.

155 Benjamin Mauk and Dan Novgorodoff, "Weather Reports: Voices from Xinjiang," *Believer Magazine*, October 1, 2019, https://www.thebeliever.net/weather-reports-voices-from-xinjiang/.

156 Phoebe Zhang, Kecheng Zhang, and Nian Yang, "Fear of data misuse as health code turns red for Chinese bank protesters," *South China Morning Post*, June 14, 2022, https://www.scmp.com/news/china/science/article/3181635/chinese-health-code-turns-red-financial-victims-about-protest.

157 "Giving Credit 2: Carrots and Sticks," *China Law Translate*, December 15, 2017, https://www.chinalawtranslate.com/en/giving-credit-2-carrots-and-sticks/.

158 Martin Hellman, one of the early co-creators of public key cryptography, faced up to ten years in jail for publishing his research.

159 Eric Hughes, "A Cypherpunk's Manifesto," Satoshi Nakamoto Institute, March 9, 1993, https://nakamotoinstitute.org/cypherpunk-manifesto/.

160 "Bernstein v. US Department of Justice," Electronic Frontier Foundation, January 29, 2024, https://www.eff.org/cases/bernstein-v-us-dept-justice.

161 "U.S. Citizen Who Conspired to Assist North Korea in Evading Sanctions Sentenced to Over Five Years and Fined $100000," Department of Justice, April 12, 2022, https://www

.justice.gov/opa/pr/us-citizen-who-conspired-assist-north-korea-evading-sanctions-sentenced-over-five-years-and.

162 James Griffiths, "China censorship: World internet freedom declines for 8th year in a row," *CNN*, November 2, 2018, https://www.cnn.com/2018/11/01/asia/internet-freedom-china-censorship-intl/index.html.

163 Yogita Khatri, "Venezuelan military officials seize 315 Bitcoin miners," *The Block*, July 8, 2020, https://www.theblock.co/linked/70744/venezuelan-military-officials-seize-315-Bitcoin-miners.

164 Michael J. Casey, "Iran's Bitcoin Bet and the Money Wars to Come," *CoinDesk*, April 30, 2021, https://www.coindesk.com/markets/2021/04/30/irans-Bitcoin-bet-and-the-money-wars-to-come/.

165 Nikhilesh Anthony, "Nigerians' Rejection of Their CBDC Is a Cautionary Tale for Other Countries," *CoinDesk*, March 6, 2023, https://www.coindesk.com/consensus-magazine/2023/03/06/nigerians-rejection-of-their-cbdc-is-a-cautionary-tale-for-other-countries/.

166 Jeremie Ree, "Five Observations on Nigeria's Central Bank Digital Currency," International Monetary Fund, November 16, 2021, https://www.imf.org/en/News/Articles/2021/11/15/na111621-five-observations-on-nigerias-central-bank-digital-currency.

167 Daniel Nguyen, "Bitcoin Adoption in Venezuela Makes It Unique Among Crisis Nations," *CoinDesk*, November 11, 2020, https://www.coindesk.com/business/2020/11/11/venezuelas-Bitcoin-story-puts-it-in-a-category-of-one/.

168 Leigh Cuen, "New Data Gives Unprecedented Insight Into How Iranians Use Bitcoin," *CoinDesk*, September 11, 2019, https://www.coindesk.com/markets/2019/09/11/new-data-gives-unprecedented-insight-into-how-iranians-use-Bitcoin/.

169 "Inflation, consumer prices (annual %) - Nigeria | Data," World Bank Open Data, February 2, 2024, https://data

.worldbank.org/indicator/FP.CPI.TOTL.ZG?locations=NG.

170 Evan Parker, "'Basically a Savior': Why Crypto Is So Popular in Turkey," *CoinDesk*, October 25, 2022. Retrieved January 29, 2024, https://www.coindesk.com/layer2/2022/10/25 /turkey-cryptocurrency-explained/.

171 Avi Singh, "Blockchain Australia Denounces Recent Banking Restrictions on Crypto Payments," *CoinDesk*, June 14, 2023, https://www.coindesk.com/policy/2023/06/14 /australias-crypto-industry-body-denounces-recent -banking-restrictions/.

172 Echo Huang, "Taiwan's new digital minister is a transgender software programmer who wants to make government more open," *Quartz*, August 26, 2016, https:// qz.com/767298/taiwans-new-digital-minister-is-a -transgender-software-programmer-who-wants-to -make-government-more-open.

173 Duncan Miriri, "Kenya's central bank says it is resolute on inflation, sees robust economic growth," *Financial Post*, May 31, 2022, https://financialpost.com/pmn/business -pmn-kenyas-central-bank-says-it-is-resolute-on-inflation -sees-robust-economic-growth-2.

174 "Let the Kenya shilling float against US dollar - Nairobi," The Star, June 22, 2022, https://www.the-star.co.ke /opinion/leader/2022-06-22-let-the-kenya-shilling-float -against-us-dollar/.

175 Mariela Antonia Bautista, "Mexico: Cash is Alive and Well," *Cash Essentials*, February 2, 2024, https://cashessentials .org/mexico-cash-is-alive-and-well/.

176 "Mexico central bank swats down banking magnate over Bitcoin," *AP*, June 28, 2021, https://apnews.com/article /caribbean-mexico-technology-bitcoin-business-52e4832f4 c47cf6ad9bc18d5d2211ed9.

177 Samson Mow, "The First Major Bitcoin Civil War," *Bitcoin Magazine*, August 1, 2022, https://Bitcoinmagazine.com /business/the-first-major-Bitcoin-civil-war.

178 Ree, "Five Observations."

About the Author

Roger Huang has been writing, thinking about, and exploring Bitcoin since 2013. A fluent Mandarin speaker who closely follows news out of China, he has been published in *TechCrunch*, *Forbes*, *VentureBeat*, *Entrepreneur*, the *Hong Kong Free Press*, the *Toronto Star*, the *Los Angeles Review of Books*, and cited in *AP*, *Wired*, and other outlets related to Bitcoin and tech developments in China. His writing has covered everything from the rise of the digital yuan to Hong Kong's protest movement, and he is a leading voice on the intersection of the Chinese state with open source freedoms.